The Terrible Tuesday

Alana Corry

BALBOA.
PRESS

A DIVISION OF HAY HOUSE

Balboa Press books may be ordered through booksellers or by contacting:

Balboa Press
A Division of Hay House
1663 Liberty Drive
Bloomington, IN 47403
www.balboapress.com
1 (877) 407-4847

Because of the dynamic nature of the Internet, any web addresses or links contained in this book may have changed since publication and may no longer be valid. The views expressed in this work are solely those of the author and do not necessarily reflect the views of the publisher, and the publisher hereby disclaims any responsibility for them.

The author of this book does not dispense medical advice or prescribe the use of any technique as a form of treatment for physical, emotional, or medical problems without the advice of a physician, either directly or indirectly. The intent of the author is only to offer information of a general nature to help you in your quest for emotional and spiritual well-being. In the event you use any of the information in this book for yourself, which is your constitutional right, the author and the publisher assume no responsibility for your actions.

Any people depicted in stock imagery provided by Thinkstock are models, and such images are being used for illustrative purposes only.
Certain stock imagery © Thinkstock.

Print information available on the last page.

ISBN: 978-1-5043-9231-0 (sc)
ISBN: 978-1-5043-9233-4 (hc)
ISBN: 978-1-5043-9232-7 (e)

Library of Congress Control Number: 2017918288

Balboa Press rev. date: 12/06/2017

Contents

Dedication

For Judy
She found me in the dark abyss
With eyes that had no light
She sat with me and stayed awhile
Until my eyes turned bright
She took me to the crossroads
And gently showed the way
The road ahead paved with light
Leading to a better day..
With love and gratitude..

Acknowledgements

I would graciously like to thank all my family and friends for their support, encouragement, understanding and patience with me on the ever winding road that has been my recovery from the terrible Tuesday. It has been a nightmare journey at times and I have been so blessed to have the support of my incredible family and wonderful friends throughout each and every stage of it. My life is rich with you in it and I am indebted to you all.

I would like to thank all the people involved in this story, the professionals, the police service, the haven, the legal team and victim support for their dedication and commitment to their chosen profession. It truly is a road less travelled and I am grateful to you all for walking it with me.

A massive thank you for all the local support I have received in my home town, the therapy, reflexology, shamanic practice, massage, angel therapy, IET, yoga and meditation- each and every one played its part in my recovery and I continue to benefit from it to this day. I am also thankful for all the spiritual assistance I have received over the years and take comfort in the knowledge that I am never really alone, no matter what the day brings.

Thank you to Balboa Press for the support on the journey to publication- especially to Walter and Sarah.

A special mention must go out to the fabulously talented Geralyn Mulqueen- for the artwork and for everything else.

I am truly grateful to my brother- for the gift that was Charlie Brown.

Para mi Hermana, con profunda gratitud por compartir verdaderamente el horror de ese horrible dia and por todos los dias desde entonces.. estaria perdido si ti..

To my P man- a huge thank-you for putting up with me in general, for the love that we share and mostly for the two little blessings that fill our days (and nights) with mayhem and madness.

I owe my deepest gratitude to my two children, who I love and adore with every fibre of my being. Their very presence in my life fills my days with light and my heart with love.

My final thanks goes out to You- the reader- if you have survived a terrible Tuesday of your own or ever found yourself at rock bottom- then I hope you find some comfort here.

PART ONE
The Act

I shall be telling this with a sigh
Somewhere ages and ages hence:
Two roads diverged in a wood, and I—
I took the one less travelled by,
And that has made all the difference.

> Robert Frost, 'The Road Not Taken'

Chapter One

As soon as I entered the room I felt a sense of calm. I looked at her and it washed over me, warming me right down to my toes. I inwardly congratulated myself for making it through another week of hell. A sigh of relief escaped me as I sat there for a moment and said nothing, taking a couple of deep breaths to prepare myself for what might come into my mind and out of my mouth. It usually surprised me, surprised and horrified me in equal measure. I was undecided which was worse: having these thoughts in my head at all or speaking them aloud. I'd concluded it was the combination that has been my undoing so far. The calmness I savoured quickly disappeared the moment I started talking, eaten by a jumble of words, and the panic that stayed hidden most of the time bubbled to the surface and spilled over.

My chair wasn't the only one in the room; opposite me was an almost identical cream leather one. Mine, however, could swivel, and this gave me something to do while I thought of something, anything, to say. All week I worried about what I would say. What we would talk about. How bad it would be. I went over and over it all in my head from one appointment to the next, but I was incapable of coming up with a plan to save me from the angst. It usually didn't take too long until something random popped into my head, something I didn't even realise I was thinking about. The problem was, once it came out of my mouth it became real and warranted further discussion, and it was this aspect which concerned me most. Judy never actually gave me the answer to any of the deep questions that came out of my mouth but, far more valuably, put my words in a concise order to gently direct me. Without her I was completely unable to make sense of most things.

The walls, like the chairs, were cream and there was a small wooden table just to the side of us. Judy sat opposite me in her chair, not too close as I have a serious issue with space, but she knew that without having to be told. I sat with my back to the door which sent my anxiety levels up another notch if that were even possible. She reassured me that no one would enter, though I can't help but feel extremely uncomfortable. 'There are stairs up to the room, and we would hear if someone was coming,' Judy said. I ignored this, and quickly scrambled to think of an escape route. How could we get out if there was a fire or if, God forbid, someone was to come up the stairs? There was only one exit and it could easily be barred. I was fully aware of my irrational thinking, but I could hardly breathe with the notion of escaping in my head along with everything else.

I took my coat off, made myself comfortable, swivelled in my chair and looked out the window – anywhere but at her until we started talking. I brought a latte with me and took a couple of sips to help settle me. All I really wanted to do was light up but I had a sneaking suspicion she wouldn't approve. The light hurt my eyes as I took off my sunglasses. I couldn't remember the last time I'd slept for more than an hour or two at a time, and I was relying on a steady stream of caffeine and nicotine to keep me going. I glanced again at the window. It was small with stained glass that would be impossible to break if I needed to. For the first time I noticed how much green glass the pattern contained, and it amazed me that it had taken seven long months to notice something so simple. I looked around the room and asked if Judy had got a new picture that I'd also just noticed hanging on the wall. Judy told me it had always been there, and it slowly sank in that I couldn't even see things that were right in front of me. I sipped my coffee and placed my hand on my stomach, inwardly telling it to calm down, to stop jumping. There was nothing to worry about in this room, but even my own stomach didn't believe me. The most familiar thought entered my mind: How? How did this happen to me? How did I end up here? In psychotherapy at a health and well-being centre in my home town in the north-west of Ireland. The only place I left the house to go.

———⁓ᴡⱺ⌒ⱻⱵⱺⱵⱻⱺⱺᴡ———

This wasn't how I imagined I would spend the last of my twenties. I was in my twenty-ninth year and should have been in London at work, going out, having fun or maybe even planning a holiday – basically continuing to do all the things that came second nature to me before The Terrible Tuesday. I imagined I would come home, settle down and have sense one day! You know – that maybe when I turned thirty I would feel the need for a mortgage, a husband, a horse or something; perhaps my biological clock would start ticking and I would want a baby. That was my aim: to wise up and get a plan when I turned thirty. Probably not the brightest idea but I was just going with the flow. It all went to shit anyway, the lovely non-plan I had for my life. Now my life was consumed with objectives, a daily ritual and agenda. This was necessary to simply get me through the day in one piece. Then there was the plan for the dark hours, it was in a league of its own for they were truly the worst.

Technically, I spent half my twenty-eighth year right here in my home town, although it was a bit like the light was on but nobody was home, so I wasn't sure it counted. Of course, I *know* how I ended up here, and initially I was grateful. In the beginning I was grateful for everything – overjoyed to be alive and breathing! Grateful He didn't squeeze His hands just that little tighter around my throat because then I wouldn't have had the luxury of complaining about having to sit here at all. It was funny really, because without Judy I would probably be sitting in some nuthouse drugged up on copious amount of Valium, chain-smoking and refusing to wash. I was grateful I wasn't. That's the way it goes though, I heard. It worked in phases, like grief. The grateful phase unfortunately only lasted until the shock wore off. Now here we were firmly in the pissed-off phase and I desperately hoped it wouldn't take too much longer to pass.

How long had I been coming here? Exactly how long was it since The Terrible Tuesday? I stopped counting after the twenty-seventh week. The truth of the matter was that time simply had no meaning for me any more and was pointless to continue counting. My existence revolved around getting through one Tuesday only to make it to the next one. I usually chain-smoked and drank tea until it was time to make the journey to my appointment – all part of the agenda, of course.

By ten o'clock in the morning it was all over and only just beginning. I stared relentlessly at the kitchen clock until it reached one minute past ten and then it was all over for another day. It was difficult to describe what actually happened when I was watching the clock. Everything was in slow motion. Each tick was loud and unmerciful yet necessary as every one brought me a step closer to being free. I tried not to concentrate on the panicked feeling in my stomach and how my breath caught in my dry throat. For the love of God, don't throw up. The only way I could describe it was like walking uphill on a really windy day when you can't get enough air into your lungs, and you know the faster you breathe the worse you make it but it's no use; short, shallow gulps are all you can manage, and you lose the ability to regulate the air in and out of your body. It stuck in my throat making it impossible to breathe out properly, but still all I could focus on was the clock on the wall. I forced myself to try and look at something else but my eyes had a mind of their own and inevitably shifted back to the dreaded clock face. In the end I gave up and just watched the time moving on at a snail's pace until one minute past ten.

Life continued on around me in the kitchen, and to reduce the clock-watching episodes my father attempted small talk. A man of few words usually, my father, so I knew it was difficult for him, but he invariably started with something about my agenda for the day. It was the strangest thing: I could hear him speak to me but his words seemed to bounce back to him without ever reaching me. It was too difficult to even comprehend formulating an appropriate answer in my head never mind speak aloud, and it didn't take him long to realise I do better with yes or no questions. I could manage a yes or a no before reverting to the clock. Ultimately, we watched the clock together, mostly in silence. Then, at ten o'clock, he turned to me asking if I was all right and I said, 'Yes, Daddy.'

My mother, ironically enough, was as regular as clockwork. She tried to entice me into eating breakfast during the nightmare hour of nine to ten, usually suggesting some form of eggs first. When that list was exhausted she expertly progressed on to the more 'bready' type breakfasts, of which there were quite a few variations in our house to go through – Even the neighbours baked bread, sent over in an effort to get me to eat, and although a kind and thoughtful gesture I couldn't eat anything at this time of the morning.

A pattern formed: I couldn't answer her relentless line of enquiry unless it was a simple and direct question. Sometimes even this became too complex for me and I answered at the wrong time. Hiding her frustration, she would declare, 'Well, I haven't even asked you a question yet.' I said no to everything anyway. What a pointless exercise designed to drive me even crazier than I already felt. What would she say if I finally found my voice and told her, 'No, I don't want any bloody breakfast, Mummy. I'm currently trying to push the maximum amount of air possible through the tiniest hole in my throat which seems to have practically closed. Luckily enough, just enough air is going through to stop me passing out at the table. My stomach is about to fall out my arse, and at the moment I can't even possibly entertain the thought of eating because that would require me to chew and swallow. To do that I would need saliva in my mouth, of which there is none, and I'm just trying not to have a nervous breakdown, so thank you very much but I will pass on the breakfast just now if you don't mind!'

Maybe she would have stopped asking sooner if I had said this, but I never said a word other than no, and she eventually stopped asking. Thinking rationally about it, in numerous discussions in my cream chair, I knew Mummy was only trying to engage me in conversation and thought me being angry with her and her suggestions was much better than blankly staring at the clock. She was just trying to get me to feel something, to be something other than the vague, empty, panic-stricken person sitting at the table. I could understand that. A mother's instinct is to feed her child and that was all she was trying to do, feed me.

Once ten o'clock came and went I relaxed a bit. Well, as much as I could under the circumstances. I maybe took a cup of tea outside and always had a well-deserved cigarette or two depending on the size of the cup. The next item on the agenda was to shower. I could cope with not washing and being a bit smelly, but I had become obsessed with my hair. It never felt clean and I had to limit myself to washing it once a day, a difficult task. I worried it was going to fall out and, unsurprisingly enough, I wouldn't have coped well with going bald on top of everything else; I have an unforgivingly large, round head that would simply not lend itself to baldness. It was unbelievable that out of everything clean hair had become my compulsion. Maybe it was because I had a dressing gown tied round my head for an hour while I sweated uncontrollably and struggled to breathe. When I finally got the damn thing off I felt like my head was going to fall off with it. You don't realise how heavy dressing gowns are until you're in a sticky predicament with one. My hair was soaked with sweat and I didn't get to wash it until I had a shower at the clinic six hours later.

So off I went, telling everyone in my path, at least five times, where precisely I was headed in case they walked into the bathroom. I had to leave the door open, and if someone walked in I would probably pass out. For about six months I never looked at myself in the mirror – not when I was getting into the shower, not when I dried myself and certainly not when I dressed. Never. I felt totally detached from my body and only ever looked up when I had finished washing and dressing. I dried my hair and then meticulously checked to see if it was thin or falling out. And then came my favourite part (regardless of the weather, I might add): I put on my treasured sunglasses. I was sure people constantly thought, 'Who does she think she is wearing sunglasses in the rain?' but I honestly didn't care what people thought of me. I had no room in my head for nonsense like that and I needed the sunglasses.

They were my protection from the world, and I felt like people couldn't see me properly when I was wearing them. If you couldn't see my eyes, then you had to believe me when I said I was fine. I avoided looking at my eyes at all times. I thought of that saying: the eyes are the windows to the soul, and I wondered where my soul was when I looked in the mirror. My eyes looked like they belonged to a dead person, like someone had turned off the light behind them and all I could see was a black hole of nothingness. They certainly didn't look like mine. It freaked me out to look in the mirror and see them staring back at me, so I thought it best for me to not see them at all.

It was strange to not want to look in the mirror and to not care about what I looked like. I must have been a bit vain before The Terrible Tuesday – I cared more than I would have cared to admit about what I looked like back then. I got up at five thirty in the morning to walk to my pre-work swim and somehow managed to walk back home after my twelve-hour shift. This meant I didn't get home until around ten o'clock at night but that didn't deter me. If I had to describe myself as I was back then I would use words like confident, bubbly, attractive, kind, carefree and determined. I no longer cared about any of that now; the simple reason was because it had gone, every word was gone, and I didn't ever want it to come back. It was what got me into this mess in the first place, and being confident, attractive and carefree only made it all the more terrible.

I hated afternoon appointments. They gave my mother more time to persuade me to eat, and it was so tiring to continually refuse her. Sometimes I gave in and begrudgingly agreed to eat something. Regardless of what it was it tasted like a block of wood, and I just moved it around my mouth and spat it into kitchen roll when I could stand it in my mouth no longer. I was convinced it might get stuck in my throat and choke me to death if I attempted swallowing, and after having quite a close shave with Dr Death I wasn't in any hurry to repeat the experience. I limited myself to the odd bit of toast and this was only when absolutely necessary. It was strange that I never felt hungry when I used to love my food so much.

I never felt much of anything really, or if I did I don't remember, except the tiredness. I remember feeling constantly exhausted. I prayed for sleep to come but it eluded me. It felt like I had been on night shift for about a year coupled with no sleep during the day. My bones ached with weariness and at times it was an effort even to smoke – to lift my hand to my mouth, breathe in and out and then in again. Still, it was a task I managed to complete at least twenty times a day. The fact that I must have smelled like a giant ashtray completely escaped me. It was a very normal thing to do, was it not – to have a cup of tea and a ciggie? If nothing else, it passed another ten minutes on the clock.

Chapter Two

I tried to remember what those first few weeks were like before I had any appointments to drag myself to, before I sat in my chair and voiced all the terrible thoughts in my head. I was home about four weeks before my first appointment, but I don't recall much of how the days passed. The nights, though, are crystal clear: lots more smoking and tea drinking and telling everyone I was fine. They must have known I wasn't. I wasn't there at all. So unsure of what the hell was going on and trying very hard to hide it.

There was plenty for me to be getting on with, of course. Basic things I couldn't get my head around attempting: emptying my flat in London, sorting out bank stuff, changing addresses and, you know, sorting out the very wreckage that was my life. Honestly, I wanted nothing to do with that flat and bad karma was my righteous justification. In my eyes what had to be done with it was simple: burn everything in the bedroom – I meant everything, and throw the rest out or give it away. I didn't care what happened to any of it as long as it didn't come my direction. I didn't want it. I never wanted to think about that flat ever again never mind keep any of its contents. In the end, my boyfriend's family sorted the entire thing out, God love them.

Despite my wishes, a few things made their way over to my parent's house: the bikes that were still in their boxes in the spare room, some CDs and my two favourite wicker chairs from a lovely shop in London. That was all right by me. I figured He couldn't have sat in them anyway, but I couldn't be completely sure. He was the biggest man I'd ever seen and surely the wicker wouldn't have supported twenty stone? Well, eighteen stone, as said in the papers, but I liked to round it up to an even twenty.

Made me feel a bit better about myself. The bigger he was, the smaller I was, and the easier it was to justify to myself why I didn't fight just that little bit harder.

When I got on the plane to come home, I had nothing except the clothes I was wearing. I had no bag, no wallet, no phone, no clothes and no money. Even my mother had my passport. I felt like I was leaving my sanity in London along with all my once-valued possessions. The best part was that I didn't care about any of that stuff, all I wanted to do was go home. I wanted to get down on my knees and kiss the tarmac outside our house and never leave again. Unfortunately, I had to wait three whole days before the police said I could go home. Three fucking horrendously long days of crying, smoking and doing exactly what I was told. My mind was consumed by one thought: I just want to go home. My lovely English friends, Rachel and David, rallied round us, putting us up, feeding, watering us and not batting an eyelid while their home was invaded. I couldn't put into words how much I appreciated their support, but to me there was simply no place like home. I often wished during those three days that I could have been Dorothy from *The Wizard of Oz*. I'd have given my right arm for a pair of magic red shoes that would have spared me the looming plane journey.

The house was never quiet for the first few weeks I was home. There were lots of visitors, lots of parties, lots of barbecues and lots of drinking. Everyone was just so relieved I was alive and in one piece. The thought of what could have been was much worse for them than the reality of what had happened. For me, it was the opposite: the reality of it was impossible for me to process. I didn't know how I could live with the horror of it all, or how I could keep it in my head forever. It didn't seem to belong to me, and it disturbed everything else no matter how insignificant. It had no place to call home in my head. I was in a quiet state of disbelief that it had happened to me – I mean really, truly, actually happened to me. I was on the outside of the celebrations. I couldn't even let myself have a drink so terrified was I that I would find myself at the bottom of a never-ending bottle, that alcohol would become my biggest problem. Quite frankly, I had enough fucking problems without adding anything else into the mix. The days rolled into each other and it was suddenly weeks since The Terrible Tuesday. I was never exactly sure of what day it was with one obvious exception, and it came along like a radar signal in my head, and more alarmingly my stomach which would be in absolute knots, making it impossible for me to eat or do anything except poo.

How was it possible for one person to eat so little and poo so much? I couldn't fathom it. It was also extremely unfair, all things considered, that I had to spend so much of my time in the bathroom. I hated my own and every other fucking bathroom I encountered, although it came in at a close second to the bedroom. How my family put up with the continual stream of poo with the bathroom door left wide open I'll never know. 'Jesus,' my dad would say, 'Teresa, you are seriously going to have to talk to her about closing that bathroom door. Anybody could walk down that hall! It's unbelievable, unbelievable!' Mum would try and explain that I wasn't able to close the door, that I just couldn't do it. Of course, I could hear every word they said as I had the window open too, just in case.

Being in the bathroom was bad enough, but every evening I had to attempt to get into my bed and sleep. Voluntarily getting into bed was the worst part. It's a very normal thing to do: get yourself ready for bed, get into bed and go to sleep. But it was a normal task that terrified me beyond belief. The closer it came to bedtime, the worse it became in my head and body. I shook all over, involuntarily, like you do when you're extremely cold. It came over me in surges and I couldn't control it. On top of the knots in my stomach and the feeling of not being able to catch my breath, it was the most unpleasant part of it all, and the lack of control I had over my body as well as my mind seriously disturbed me. Judy explained that it was my body's way of releasing stress – that I should consider it a positive thing. It didn't make experiencing it first-hand any fucking easier, mind you, and in my head I counted how many times people asked me the exact same thing: 'Are you cold?', 'Do you want a jumper?', 'You're shaking …'. I would hold out for as long as I could stand it – my average was about five times although I made it to eleven, but only the once. I think we all knew the jumper made no difference to the shaking but it gave people something to do, to feel like they were helping, and I often thanked God it was July and not December or I'd have been wrapped up like an Eskimo.

Eventually I just had to do it. Get into bed. That first night in my friend Rachel's house, my boyfriend, Phil, my mum and I all slept in the same bed with my brother, Paul, on the floor. (My mum and Paul had flown over earlier in the day.) I was in the middle of the bed but I couldn't stop shaking despite Mum and Phil holding onto me for dear life. Every time I lay down I would panic, hyperventilate, sit up again and exclaim, 'I can't breathe. I can't do it. I can't!' Phil tried his best to hold me to his chest and tell me a story. I had to concentrate on visualising all the things he was saying. The hope being it would calm me down enough to fall asleep. It was a beautiful story full of all my favourite things and on any other day I would have loved every minute of it. It was extraordinary, and to this day I cry thinking about it. Phil telling his story in front of Mum and my brother without a second's hesitation or sense of embarrassment makes me even more emotional. It pains me to think I never properly thanked him for trying so hard to comfort me despite the gulf that had emerged between us in the last twelve hours. In that moment though, while I was lying on his chest, I genuinely thought maybe it would be okay and just maybe we would make it through it all together. Regardless of his best efforts, I couldn't be calmed. Mum and I went back downstairs to recommence chain-smoking and tea drinking until dawn slowly arrived.

———∿∿◦◦◦◦◦◦∿∿———

In one of my first appointments Judy explained it was because I was asleep in my own bed when it happened, that's why I couldn't relax enough to even attempt sleep. Your bed is supposed to be the safest, most secure place in the world, but it is also where you are at your most vulnerable. If I had been in the kitchen frying eggs, I would have thrown the pan at Him and made a run for it, but I wasn't. I was asleep in my bed. In that situation, survival mechanisms kicked in and I did what I must to survive. Association was my biggest problem now. I associated going to bed with waking to find a huge black man at the bedroom door who jumped on me. It should be simple then, wouldn't you think? The solution: don't associate the two things. Treat them as separate, single events. Sounded easy except that I didn't know how to separate the two events in my head, and it wasn't something Judy could just tell me how to do. No one seemed able to tell me how to do it and yet people could usually tell you how to do all sorts of useless things.

All I wanted to do, more than anything in the world, was get into my own bed and go to sleep, but every time I tried I had some sort of small breakdown. It was truly terrifying but I had to work it out on my own. I decided I was going to do it. The determined side of me was back with a vengeance and it would never give up. It wasn't like I had much choice in the matter. I mean, I had to sleep again sometime, right? Well, watch this space, people, because I'm going to work it out and then I'm going to tell everyone how to do it.

Judy told me that my awareness was heightened because my safety boundaries had been broken by the unexpectedness of it. I had quite simply lost my peace of mind. That made perfect sense. No one walked around expecting those things to happen – you didn't expect to be mugged, attacked or have your house broken into and be jumped on when you're asleep. It's the element of surprise that gives the bastards an advantage over you, and because of this your reaction times are obviously compromised. By the time I had caught up with his plan, it was far too late to do anything about it. It would have been much nicer of Him if He had politely knocked on the door, told me His plan and then given me a few minutes to get ready for it, by which time I would have legged it out the back door and over the garden wall. It was a waste of time thinking like that because that wasn't how it happened and I couldn't change it. I had lost my peace of mind and I couldn't get into bed, couldn't sleep, couldn't eat and I stared at the clock. I had lost my peace of mind and I didn't even know I had it until it was gone.

I took for granted – like every other normal person on this planet – that things like that just didn't happen to people like me. It just didn't. Nothing like this had ever happened to anyone I knew and I knew a fair number of people. Sure, I'd heard it on the news and read about it in the newspaper, but thankfully it just didn't affect me. I never thought about it in any real capacity. I'm a nurse and spent my days looking after children who were seriously ill. I liked to think of myself as a kind and generous person, and while not overly religious I was quite spiritual – I'd always been aware of a spiritual presence in my life. Although raised a Roman Catholic I'd never felt an innate need to spend much time at Mass, unlike many I knew and loved for whom Mass is almost a second home. If God was within us and around us, then surely he didn't care where or how we prayed to him. My mother said this was how I eased my conscience over not practising religion, and that I couldn't pick and choose the parts of

Catholicism that suited me best, so I decided I wasn't really meant to be a Catholic. Despite this, however, I always felt a close affinity to Padre Pio, a saint my mother prayed to often. I followed her example and felt he was watching over me. At times of serious doubt I prayed hard and felt him with me – could smell the flowery scent that is said to come from him. I felt such peace in those moments that I was under the illusion I would continue to breeze through life without any problems or life-shattering incidents. Bad things didn't happen to good people like me, they just didn't. Jesus, what a rude awakening.

It was funny how I noticed the word everywhere I went. It was in every newspaper and on every news channel and radio station. Magazine covers with some poor soul telling her survival story shouted it at me in the shops. I couldn't seem to escape it and it just wasn't right. That word shouldn't be in my head. RAPE. Four simple letters that when put together as a word took on a whole new meaning for me. It was a horrible, disgusting, dirty, shameful word. The sound of it brought bile to the back of my throat, made my pupils dilate and the breath catch in my lungs. It made me shake with fear and helplessness – not just the word, but the horrible memories that went along with it.

The memories were the real problem. That the word meant something to me now made me both excruciatingly sad and violently angry. Before The Terrible Tuesday I would never have bought a magazine with that story on the cover. I admit, I wasn't interested in other people's horror stories. I would read the headline and turn the page. Maybe I was selfish, I don't know, but it's like child abuse or paedophilia – even if you read about it or see it on television, it doesn't really touch you. You think to yourself, 'Jesus, that's terrible!' but then you go straight back to worrying about where you put your car keys or what you're making for dinner.

About two months into our sessions Judy pointed out that He wasn't *just* a burglar, which would have been bad enough. Burglars, by nature, steal things, usually when you're not in your own home, and many a burglar, apparently, would be disgusted at his behaviour towards me. He is a rapist as well as a burglar, she told me. Fucking charming, that's what that is. I couldn't believe I was incapable of coming to that conclusion myself, that if it wasn't for my psychotherapist I may never have connected the dots. My brain wasn't working correctly but the sense of clarity was overwhelming and it made perfect sense when Judy explained it. It was just another one of those things I never gave too much thought to before – the different criminals there are in this world. I felt like I'd been dropped onto a different planet, one I didn't like or recognise at all.

Chapter Three

At my very first appointment nerves took over in a way I couldn't even fathom. It was as though I was learning to walk again. I didn't remember arriving at the centre, going up the stairs or the pair of us introducing ourselves. The first thing I properly recalled was Judy asking me what I hoped to gain from being there. I laughed. Pretty serious question for someone as fucked up as me. I could barely spell my own name let alone articulate an intelligent answer, but I gave it a whirl and tried to make her understand in the simplest of terms that the memories of The Terrible Tuesday had nowhere to go – they didn't fit inside my head. The whole escapade was just not supposed to be in there and I didn't know what to do with it. Judy said that the objective was for The Terrible Tuesday not to have central focus in my life. Central focus. I liked that phrase. I liked it a lot. It made sense to me – something I hadn't been able to say for quite a while. I didn't want the rest of my life to revolve around this one day, but, to my knowledge, the whole purpose of setting an objective was that it was realistic and achievable, and if Judy thought her objective seemed realistic or achievable to me, she was very seriously mistaken. For this experience not to have central focus in my life would be nothing short of a fucking miracle.

She asked what had happened, for me to take her through The Terrible Tuesday. 'Sure,' I said. 'No problem.' Only it was a problem, a *big* problem. To verbalise what happened I must relive it in my head. It wasn't like trying to remember the details of a film – I actually had to feel it and experience it, live through it again even, every fucking nanosecond of it as painful and terrifying as the first time. Apart from the police and Rachel, who was with me on The Terrible Tuesday, I'd tried not to tell anyone the details if I could help it.

Thinking back to that first day at the centre, I realise I was at a holiday camp in my head called denial. Everyone should go there at some point, even for a short stay. My favourite word was peachy. People would ask how I was and I would say, 'Peachy!' Did I honestly think anyone believed me? I told myself I was fine repeatedly – maybe a hundred times a day: I am fine, I am fine, I am fine, I am fine. I thought if I told myself often enough, it would come true. I was sure I was fine until it was just me and Judy sitting in the chairs and she asked me, 'How are you really? Are you really fine?' and then suddenly I wasn't so sure. I didn't really know how to answer and I didn't want to cry.

Not only that, but I wasn't so sure I could tell her what had happened. I could try but, honestly, it was pretty excruciating looking someone in the eye and sharing your worst moments. There was something truly painful about it and I wished she could just hold my hand and read my mind. I wished she could find out without me having to tell her.

I guess I wasn't used to the shift in power in my relationship with Judy; the title of professional was usually bestowed on me. I worked on a ward with extremely sick children, and I'd helped many a child pass over into the next life and many a parent make it through their child's final hours. I was the one in control of the situation, the comforter, the organiser, the go-to person. It was a difficult job but I love it and I'd been consumed by it for six years. The role reversal was a bitter pill to swallow and I was suddenly very much aware that it was *rock-fucking-bottom* for me. I was totally, completely and utterly broken.

Those moments when I thought I was going to die, the fear was overwhelming. Did all those children feel what I felt? I sincerely hope they didn't. I did my best to ensure they felt no pain. What about their parents? Was the desperation, panic and loss what they felt too? Is being broken the same for everyone regardless of the route you take to get there? Work was the only other really emotive situation I had ever experienced or could compare this to. I couldn't get my head round the fact that the coin had flipped for me and that I was very much on the other side. Was Judy going to try and do for me what I tried to do for the children and parents at the hospital? More importantly, was I going to let her? Did I just get on the train to no man's land, and, if so, how the fuck did I get off?

Trying to maintain a sense of professionalism with her wasn't going to get me very far, yet I was reluctant to burden her with the horror of it all. She seemed like a nice, decent woman, and I didn't know anything about her. I didn't want to single-handedly destroy whatever concept she had of the world and the people in it. I knew my mother had given her a rundown of the situation when booking me in, and I was reassured and pleasantly surprised that she hadn't given me *the look* which happened when someone who had heard of The Terrible Tuesday ran into me for the first time. Judy may be the first person I had talked to in the last month or so who hadn't looked at me with a mixture of pity and total bewilderment, whose look hadn't said I want to ask how you are but if you start talking to me about it I will die on the spot and won't know what to say. People had ignored me or pretended they hadn't seen me and I didn't blame them in the slightest – I wouldn't know what to say to me either. Perhaps I could just be a normal person in here with someone who hadn't subjected me to *the look*. Either way, Judy told me she could protect herself from it all and that it was okay, I could go ahead. Right. No problem. Fuck.

—⁓⦿⦿⦿⦿⁓—

It was after one in the morning when I made it into the flat having been home in Ireland for my close friend's hen party. I was a bridesmaid and, naturally, the chief party planner. We'd already been to Barcelona – what a weekend that was, and I flew to England on the last flight from Belfast International to Stansted, delayed for hours (nothing new there), hungover, knackered and grumpy. Come Tuesday morning I woke with a blinding headache, so I phoned work and told the girls I wouldn't be in until the afternoon hoping that more sleep would rid me of my migraine. It was unbelievable that the morning I chose to take some time owing would be the worst morning in the world to be in my bed. Unlucky didn't begin to cover it.

The last thing I remember was Phil waking me to ask where his shin pads where. He had this annoying habit of waking me each morning to ask the whereabouts of something that was usually right in front of him. 'Get out,' I said. Can you imagine the utter awfulness of it if those had been my last words to another human being on this planet? I've thought about that quite often. Perhaps even worse, is that how he would have remembered me? I wasn't aware he had worked from home that morning and that it was already nearly nine o'clock. He left for work on his bike and recalled seeing a black man sitting in a car behind the bin lorry outside our flat. The criminal behind the wheel saw Phil leave, parked up and broke into our flat while I was asleep in our bed.

In my semi-conscious state I was vaguely aware of some noise but I put it down to the new neighbours who had been installing soundproofing. I didn't pay much attention to the noise – the first of my mistakes. I then heard footsteps running down the hall, heavy footsteps, really heavy, in fact, and I thought they didn't sound like Phil's, yet I remained in my bed – mistake number two. In my sleepy state I tried to sit up, and that was when the bedroom door opened and I caught a quick look at Him. Huge. Black. He jumped on me, shouting orders, 'Don't fucking look at me! Close your eyes! Why didn't you answer the fucking door? Who else is in the house?' He roared. On and on the questions went and I obviously wasn't capable of thinking straight. He lifted Phil's dressing gown, a thick, grey, towelling robe and put it over my head and around the front of my neck. It hit me then, like a ton of fucking bricks being dropped into my stomach. Shit. What the fuck was he doing in my house and how the fuck was I going to get out? I realised I was in danger and started to shake uncontrollably. I was hyperventilating and the robe was so thick I just couldn't seem to get enough air into my lungs. I was going to pass out. Jesus Christ, he is going to suffocate me! I thought.

He was on top of me on the bed with His knees on my back and His hands pressing my head down into the bed. He was so heavy. 'Calm down and listen to me. I am not going to hurt you. I am not going to rape you. I just want your money.' He continued, 'Stop breathing like that. Just calm down. I am not going to hurt you as long as you do everything that I tell you.' He soon realised that I couldn't be calmed and decided on a different strategy. 'Shut the fuck up or I will really hurt you!' That tactic worked a bit better. I tried really hard to be quiet. I don't know if you've ever tried to be quiet when you are utterly panic-stricken but take my word for it, it's virtually impossible. It was a simple command really: just don't make any noise. Unfortunately for me, my body and vocal chords had a mind of their own. My breathing was excruciatingly loud. We went around the flat, Him holding me at the back of my neck as he carelessly pushed me into walls and doors. I couldn't see never mind fucking think straight and definitely not enough to simply let my feet do the walking for me. I felt no pain with all the banging and the crashing into things, I was frozen with fear. He shouted at me the whole time, 'Make a fucking sound and I will kill you. Make a run for it and I will kill you.' Anything at all it seemed would result in me being killed. We closed the front door then got my bag and wallet. He manoeuvred me back into the bedroom where He told me to lie on my stomach on the bed. He didn't have to hold me down this time, I was too terrified to move.

Bank cards, pin numbers – that's all that mattered. He called me Alana like he had a right to use my first name and as though we were having a normal, everyday conversation. I gave Him everything he asked for but I couldn't remember the pin number for my credit card. I'd never used it before and I'd only recently received it, rendering me incapable of remembering my pin. That wasn't good enough for Him. 'Maybe it's in the drawer,' I reasoned. He was in the process of trashing my bedroom, looking for God knows what. My hearing seemed to have moved up a couple of notches to the point of almost super-power status as my sight was taken from me. Every sound was so clear and I tried to make sense of what He was doing and where He was in the room. I used my hands and loosened the robe so I could see the contents of the drawer and then it came to me: *9444*. Relief. I told Him where He would find a statement with an available balance of three thousand pounds. My brain finally woke up. *Welcome to the fucking party, Alana!* 'If you open the wardrobe and give me a pair of trousers, I'll get dressed and come to the shop with you. I'll get you any amount of money you want,' I said. I knew there was no other way out.

He was too big for me to fight but I just might have been able to persuade Him to take me outside. He didn't sound too clever, not by his use of the English language anyway, but I knew there were many ways to be clever. It became apparent that my only chance of survival was to talk my way out. He asked me where the trousers were and I told Him they were in the wardrobe. I pleaded with Him, telling Him I would simply withdraw the money and give it to Him. I wouldn't scream or shout because I knew He must really need it. He thought about it. He almost bought it and then decided against it. So acute was my disappointment I almost vomited. That was my only chance to escape and I knew it.

He shoved me back into the bed and held my head into the pillows just to reinforce his power and total control over the situation. 'Shut the fuck up,' He said. 'No one is going anywhere! You'll scream, shout and make a run for it. I'm not stupid, you know?' Over and over again: 'WHAT ARE THE PIN NUMBERS? WHAT ARE THE PIN NUMBERS? WHAT ARE THE PIN NUMBERS?' He wrote them down. I could hardly speak my mouth was so dry and I was so uncomfortable in just my nightshirt. I just wanted to put on some trousers. I wasn't wearing any underwear. He dragged me back up off the bed, shoving me into walls, stumbling around the flat and into my flatmate Emma's room looking for jewellery, a laptop or spare cash.

'I'm a nurse! I don't have any money and I don't have a laptop!' I reasoned.

Everything I told Him was the truth as the shock of what was happening left me unable to lie. Back in the bedroom I resumed my position of lying on my stomach. He went through Phil's drawers on the right side of the bed asking me who Phil was and when he'd be home from work. Phil wasn't due home until around three o'clock, and He said we would wait until then so Phil could give Him the money. Jesus Christ. I had no idea what time it was but I knew I couldn't possibly cope with this shit until three o'clock. He would kill Phil as soon as he came through the door.

'Look, I promise you, I've given you everything I have,' I said. 'I don't tell lies and I have no reason to lie to you. I just want to go home.'

'You are home,' He responded.

'No,' I told Him. 'I don't come from here. I just want to go home to Ireland, to my family!'

'Shut the fuck up,' He said, laughing at me.

I tried to pull my nightshirt down a bit – I felt so exposed, but I couldn't see whether He was looking at me or not. 'Stop that and don't fucking move! I didn't tell you you could do that, did I? Don't fucking cover yourself. Don't fucking do anything unless I tell you.'

Chapter Four

'Get up ... I said, get the fuck up!' He shouted as He moved me to the other side of the bed. I went to lie on my stomach and He demanded I lie on my back instead. Everything considered, I thought maybe I could be forgiven for being a tad confused as to which side was which and for not moving quick enough for Him. It was a miracle I was moving at all. My heart was beating so loud and so fast I thought it would explode out of my chest at any minute.

I just knew He had seen the condoms in Phil's drawer. I was so terrified I thought I was going to wet myself. His phone rang. 'Shit!' He said and switched it off. He stood on phones and turned over the lamps. 'You're not going to make a sound. I need to get to the bank for the money.' He tried to tie my legs together with cord but the task proved too difficult for Him as my legs were shaking with such speed and it was impossible for me to keep them still.

He almost left then. He was still shouting at me but his voice was moving further and further away. I heard His footsteps on the wooden floor in the hallway and I almost relaxed. I desperately tried to hold my breath so I could hear Him better. I couldn't believe He was leaving. Maybe someone was waiting for Him outside and it was them on the phone? 'Ah, fuck it,' he said, 'I may as well have a quick go while I'm here.'

It took far longer than it should have for me to understand the meaning of that sentence. Good old denial kicks in when you need it most. All I could hear next was His zip coming down as He moved towards the drawer and opened it. Then the sound I had been dreading most, the opening of a condom wrapper. 'You don't have to do that!' I pleaded. 'Please, please don't! Please! Please don't!' I might have said it fifty times over. I knew it

23

was pointless but I just kept repeating myself. We both knew He wasn't going to change his mind. The pain in my chest was so intense, my head was dizzy and I knew I wasn't breathing in enough air. My whole body was shaking but I was frozen with fear. I couldn't move an inch. I am going to die. Right here on this bed. I am going to die. I can't. I just can't die like this. This can't be it. The last thing I said to Phil was 'Get out!' and that can't be the last thing I say,. It just can't. I want to go home. I want to see my little nephew, Nathan, and give him a cuddle. I want to be in my own bed with Mummy in the kitchen. I want to go to my favourite pub in my home town with the girls. I want to smoke cigarettes and drink wine with my sisters. Oh Jesus, please don't let this be it!'

'Shut the fuck up. Stop crying or I will kill you. Shut up!' He shouted repeatedly. I put my hand over my mouth to try and quiet myself but I just couldn't stop crying. 'Open your legs,' He demanded. I would have obliged but I couldn't make myself move my legs apart when every fibre of my being wanted to keep them closed. He grew impatient with me and pushed them open forcefully pulling me downwards on the bed and dragging my legs so they were firmly on the floor. He pushed himself inside me, with one hand squeezing my throat and the other roaming my body as if He had a right to touch me. Just because He could, just because He was bigger than me, stronger than me and to top it all off, just because He was a fucking criminal. These factors combined somehow gave Him all the right in the world to touch me without my permission.

I had never felt so alone in my whole life, and it was so cold in my bedroom. Had I been able to see, I would have seen my breath fill the otherwise dark room. Every short, panicky gulp that I took and every noisy breath felt like it does when you go outside in the stillness of the morning when it has snowed overnight. Evil. That's why it's so cold. The darkness was oozing out of Him and I could feel it. I just wanted to go home. God, please let me go home and see my mummy just one more time. He withdrew out of me, obviously not quite as erect as He would have liked, and made disgusting grunting noises while massaging Himself. I tried my hardest to swallow the vomit at the back of my throat, fearful of choking to death – if I choked on my own vomit, would it be His fault? Would He be responsible for my death?

He really went for it then and I thought it was never going to be over.

He was hurting me and every time He squeezed my throat I couldn't breathe. 'Please don't do that,' I croaked. 'I can't breathe.' But He didn't care. I went somewhere else in my head after that, unable to cope with it any more. That was the moment the light went out in my eyes. I am sure of that. It was just too much. There was too much fear, too much horror, too much pain. My brain just wouldn't function and felt like it had shut down completely. I didn't think about anything then except that maybe God had deserted me. Maybe I should have gone to Mass after all and where the fuck was Padre Pio when I needed him most? Did I deserve to be deserted like this? Did anyone?

When He finished He quickly resumed the shouting, 'Up. Get the fuck up. You're going to the shower.' He lifted me off the bed and half carried me to the bathroom, violently banging me into walls and doors along the way. I still couldn't move, I was helpless, and my legs had forgotten where the bathroom was. I had to climb into the bath to reach the shower, easier said than done when I still couldn't see a thing. I scrambled round desperately searching for my shower gel and cursed myself when I realised it was in my swimming bag and I would have to use Phil's. 'WHAT ARE THE PIN NUMBERS?' He bellowed relentlessly as He held me continuously under the water. The dressing gown was still over my head and sweat was running down my face. Strange for someone who doesn't sweat very much and is constantly reminded by friends how lucky I am. Well, by Christ, I was sweating now. 'Do you not know how to wash properly?' he asked snidely. Something inside me snapped. It was the final insult and I couldn't take any more. 'Of course I know how to wash but it's a bit difficult when I can't fucking see!' I said. He held me tighter under the water then. Jesus, Alana, shut the hell up before you're drowned in the fucking bath.

'You're not going to scream. I need to get to the bank with these cards. I need the money. I'm going to the bank and I will be back for you in fifteen minutes. If you make a sound or scream, I will kill you.'

'I won't do anything!' I said. 'I'll just stay here. I promise you, I won't!'

I heard the bathroom door rattle. It had an old lock and a knob on the door that had to be turned right round to open and close it. I didn't move or make a sound. I stayed under the shower for a few more minutes too terrified to even think of moving. Eventually, I turned the shower off and took the dressing gown off my head. My neck was killing me. I hung it on the back of the door and tried to turn the handle with an unsurprising lack of effort. It was locked and I could see the key wasn't in the keyhole as it should have been. I came to a sudden realisation … He has locked me in here! *Shit*. Fifteen minutes, He said. I'm as good as dead. Fifteen minutes! I have fifteen minutes to get the fuck out of here.

I knelt on the bathroom floor and looked through the keyhole. The bathroom led directly out onto a long narrow hall and then the front door. I could see the front door was open and the light was shining in. He had obviously left. I put my head on the door and panic washed over me. *Oh my God, His phone rang*. What if He brought his friends back with Him? I would rather He put a bullet in the back of my head than go through that again. I can't be in this small, windowless bathroom in fifteen minutes' time.

I looked at my watch: ten to ten. Was that all? How was that possible? I felt like He had been there for hours. I had no idea what time He came in at in the first place but it was incredible that it wasn't even ten o'clock. I looked in the bathroom cabinet and found a nail file. I remembered a film with Clint Eastwood picking locks with a hair clip. Looks easy, right? Wrong. Maybe it would work if my hands stopped shaking. It was no use. Fuck. I went to the sink, splashed some water on my face and fixed my hair. I looked in the mirror. I took a couple of deep breaths and noticed the air felt different – like someone was with me. 'Right,' I said aloud. 'I know you're here. I need some help. I need to get out of this bathroom and I need you to show me the way.' I had no idea who I was talking to – God, dead loved ones, I really didn't know, but the thought of a helpful presence in the room calmed me.

I continued searching through the bathroom cabinet and found a pair of nursing scissors. I took them over to the door. What the fuck was I going to do with these? It wasn't a conscious plan but I opened the scissors and used the edge to unscrew the bolts from the lock that went across both the door and door frame. One hand held the scissors and I held my wrist with my other hand to try and steady it enough to loosen the screws. I think I got three screws out but I was conscious of the time it was taking me to loosen each one, shaking as much as I was. I didn't want to run out of time and with ten minutes gone it was now or never.

I put one leg up on the bath, both my hands round the door handle and pulled hard. I had no idea where I got the strength from but I pulled and pulled. I heard a sound, like a growling sound, and I realised it was coming from me. I felt like I had the strength of a lion. Ignoring the pain in my arms and shoulders, I pulled until the lock came away from the wall and the door opened. I almost fell to the floor. I couldn't see properly and my head was spinning as the blood rushed through my veins and warmed me right down to my feet spurring me on. I took a giant breath in, 'Fuck you. You underestimated me. You picked the wrong flat and the wrong girl to mess with. I saw you. I saw you. Come on back and bring your friends, you fucking coward. I won't be here.' The elation I felt as I looked at the lock and the open door is hard to describe. Sweet mother of God, I did it, and I'm free and out of every part of it all, it's this part of the day which I try to hold onto in the dark hours.

———————— ∾∾◦∾◦◦◦◦◦◦◦◦∾∾ ————————

I stumbled across the hall to close the front door, still unable to get my legs working properly – feeling like they belonged to someone else, and ran with all my might down the hall and into my bedroom. I put on a pair of combats and a hoodie despite being soaking wet. Christ. What a fucking mess. Everywhere was completely trashed. Everywhere. I ran into the kitchen, pulled a chair over to stand on and reached up for the packet of smokes I kept hidden on top of the cupboard in case of emergencies. This was certainly one of those. I grabbed them and went straight to the front door without a moment's hesitation. I opened it and stopped dead. The panic hit me again. I was standing frozen at the door in the paralysing fear of getting caught. I knew the neighbours directly across the road from our flat. One of them, Mairead, had mistakenly ran over my feet with her shopping trolley at the bus stop. We soon realised we were both from Northern Ireland and became well acquainted. Mairead and the women who lived with her were nuns and the house they lived in was a convent. I'd made them soup and buns on my days off. Thank God for that. I stood there too nervous to move as I thought about making it across the road – terrified He would appear at any given second. *Fuck it, go.* I ran for my life and rang the bell. Please let someone be home. I have nowhere else to go. Please let them be in. Maria, one of the nuns, opened the door.

'Do you remember me?' I asked.

She looked at me, puzzled by my sudden appearance. 'Yes, Alana, are you all right?'

'No,' I gasped. 'I really need some help. Is Mairead here?'

Just then Mairead came down the stairs. For a moment I thought maybe I could tell her it was only a burglary, only for a spilt second, just say it was a burglary and leave out the rest. Maybe nobody would ever have to know about the other stuff? The notion didn't last long.

'A man broke into my house, Mairead,' I said. 'I need you to help me. He raped me, Mairead, he raped me, and I need you to call the police.'

'Right, darling,' she said, but I could barely make out her voice. My heart was beating so loudly it pounded in my ears and head. I couldn't stop shaking and waves of nausea kept washing over me. I tried to light a cigarette and couldn't even manage that. Mairead tried to light it for me but she put it in her mouth the wrong way round and it obviously wouldn't light. I told her it was okay, that she didn't have to do that. Even in desperate moments like those there was something so wrong seeing a nun trying to light a cigarette.

'Let's light a candle and say a prayer,' I said to her instead. I don't remember the prayer but I knew I needed to focus and badly needed to calm down. I asked Mairead again to ring the police. She looked at me.

'Right, darling, do you know the number of the police station?'

I would have laughed at this question in any other situation, I know I would have, but I was just too far gone.

'Jesus, Mairead!' I said, 'just ring 999! I think this qualifies as an emergency.'

She grabbed the phone and dialled.

The operator was in the middle of asking me a series of questions through Mairead when I lost it. Lost control. It was just too real. I retched, puked and cried uncontrollably. Once again I just couldn't stop myself. I started to shake and cried out desperately that I wanted my mummy. The operator said she would send an ambulance and the police would be there in a few minutes. She told me not to smoke or drink anything but it was too late for that as I'd already lit the fag and had a glass of water.

I phoned Phil but he didn't answer and in desperation I resorted to trying his work number instead. 'Phil? It's me,' I somehow managed to utter, but that was all. I couldn't breathe and I couldn't stop crying. I regained some composure, 'You have to come home. Someone broke into the flat. I'm at the nuns' house across the road.' I don't remember if he said anything apart from that he would be there as soon as he could. He might have asked me if I was all right or for more details but I think he knew by my voice that there was something really wrong. I'm not a person who cries easily, or at least I didn't used to be. I put the phone down. Jesus, how was I going to tell him? I couldn't tell him. I just couldn't.

I tried to call home but the line was busy. Then I called each one of my brothers, but I still couldn't reach a soul. I couldn't remember anyone's mobile number and it was driving me mad. I was usually really good with such things but they just weren't in my head. Every day since I repeat my father's mobile number over and over in my head like a mantra just in case I need it, and, well, you never know.

I was in the garden at Mairead's and it was a beautiful, warm, sunny day but I was freezing. I walked around the garden crying, retching and pulling at my hair. I could hardly stand up and was terrified. Christ, Jesus Christ, what the fuck just happened? I couldn't make sense of it. How could I have been abandoned by God and everyone in heaven? What had I ever done to deserve this? I was in shock and my mind had wandered into the unknown, probably trying to catch up with my soul which had legged it back there in the bedroom. All I was left with was a badly bruised and damaged body.

I was having a hard time focusing on what was going on around me when two police officers, Andrew and Lucy, arrived. I was at one end of the garden and kept telling them not to come too close and certainly not to touch me despite how nice they were. They asked me some basic questions.

'How are you doing?'

Seriously, wasn't it obvious how I was doing?

'I'm not so good, Andrew,' I said as I took a long drag of my cigarette. 'I mean, I've been better, you know?'

He ignored this and asked if I needed a paramedic. How could I know the answer to that? I had no idea what was going on never mind whether I was medically okay or not, but perhaps they could inject me with something to wake me from this fucking nightmare of a morning.

Chapter Five

I was worried I was late for work, but Andrew contacted them and told me not to worry about such things, that I had to concentrate on my own well-being. They asked if I had any pain anywhere, but all I could reply with was, 'I'm okay.' This couldn't have been further from the truth: I had a pain in my chest, in my neck and in my shoulders, and my head in general felt like it belonged to someone else. My arm hurt when I moved even slightly and I had a pain between my legs. It was all more of a dull ache, however, and none of it had time to reach my brain – evidenced when I told them assuredly there was no need for paramedics who came anyway, along with what seemed like a hundred more police. Even still I couldn't process what was happening.

Phil arrived, very pale and sweating. At the sight of him I cried hysterically and told everyone, right in front of him, not to tell him what had happened. I'm sure he worked it out, but even now I'm not sure who broke the news to him. It's terrible but I never really gave too much thought to the importance of it. I was so lost on the inside I couldn't possibly think of his feelings before mine. He later told me he was coming round the corner of our street on his bike when the ambulance nearly took him out.

He said it was like a movie set outside, with police cars everywhere and the whole street cordoned off with yellow tape. The police asked him to step into another room and said it would be better if Phil and I didn't talk to each other. I didn't understand it at the time but they had to eliminate him as a suspect – protocol apparently. I was told we were waiting for a specialist unit to arrive but I had no idea what that meant. In the meantime we tried to cancel my credit cards but I couldn't remember any details or passwords. Then they told me two hundred and fifty pounds had been withdrawn from my account only ten minutes previous. This brought on a fresh bout of retching, puking and crying.

I asked Phil to phone home and talk to my brother Paul first, to tell him what happened so he could tell my parents. I made him promise between retches that no matter what happened Paul had to make my daddy sit down before he broke the news. I was so worried it would be too much and would bring on a heart attack. Despite his best efforts, Phil just couldn't do it. He started crying on the phone and I ended up telling Paul myself. I don't remember too much of the conversation except Paul asking if He had a gun. Jesus, as if it wasn't bad enough without a gun. I assured him that He didn't but that he was very, very big. I became hysterical, 'He tied a dressing gown over my head and said he was going to kill me and tied me up and—'

'*Okay!*' he said in a tone that told me he didn't want to hear any more. He said to give him ten minutes and he would ring back. Phil apologised profusely, said he was so sorry, that he didn't know what had happened. I asked him to ring my friend Rachel to tell her I needed her to come to the nuns' house. I needed all the support I could get. It seemed like two minutes later the phone rang.

'Alana, this is your mother,' the soothing voice on the line said. You know, just in case I didn't know who she was. 'Everything will be fine. Everything will be ok. We will get through it,' she said reassuringly.

'Oh, Mummy!' I said, 'I feel so sick.' Hearing her voice, I knew more than ever I needed her with me. She said I wasn't to worry about a thing because she and my brother were flying over shortly. I asked her why my dad wasn't coming. He couldn't. I told her to put him on the phone immediately.

'Daddy, are you all right?'

'No, Alana, are you?' he asked.

'I'm okay, Daddy. I need to come home.'

His voice worried me. I'd only heard that tone on a few occasions in my life. It was a tone of utter despair and grave anger. He asked me questions about the police, who was there and what the plan was. The last thing I had in my head was a plan. I asked him to get my sister Anne to ring me. We were very close and I desperately needed to talk to her. Nobody could bring themselves to ask me the most obvious question of all: what happened? Not Phil, not Paul, nor my parents. In the end, even my sisters didn't ask me. I couldn't understand it. My mother was put back on the line.

'Mummy, did they tell you what he did to me?'

'They did, but you aren't to worry about that now,' she responded tearfully.

Like I had a fucking choice! The anger was building up inside me. 'Right, well I'll just put it out of my mind then, shall I?' Fuck, it was unbelievable.

I was still having to demand that Phil rang Rachel – I must have asked a hundred times. He said he couldn't get through and he was making tea for the officers. 'FUCK THE FUCKING TEA, PHIL! MAKE THE CALL!' I shouted across the kitchen.

———

I couldn't have imagined it possible, but more police arrived along with two So-Ed officers from the Sapphire Unit (I didn't realise they were police officers who specialised in sex crimes) who 'deal with this sort of thing' as they so eloquently put it. What sort of thing did they mean precisely – people who try and kill you, people who break into your home and do terrible, unspeakable things to you? Are there more people like Him just walking around pretending to be human? Oh God, it was just too awful to think about.

Anne still hadn't rung me, so I phoned my parents back. I explained again that I needed to speak to her and they said she must be in work.

'Daddy, this is a fucking emergency!' I said.

He reassured me she would ring when they got through and explained the situation to her. He tried his best to calm me, asking questions to keep my mind occupied and out of the current abyss it was in.

'Who's there, Alana? Who is with you at the moment?' he queried.

'I don't know, Daddy. The entire fucking world and its dog by the looks of it.'

Despite his best efforts, it was no use. I handed the phone back to Phil with my parents still on the line. He looked at me and told me quietly that Rachel was on her way. Finally, some good news. The phone rang – it was my sister Anne. She talked so quietly I could barely make her out.

'Jesus Christ, Anne! I've been waiting for you to ring. Where have you been? Did they tell you what he did to me? Did they? Did they?'

'You're going to be all right, Alana, I promise.'

'I thought he was going to kill me, Anne. I mean really kill me. I thought I was actually, really, going to die. Seriously, it's totally insane … Are you there? Are you listening to me at all?'

I don't know what I was expecting any of them to say to me. I was just so shocked and preoccupied dealing with my own grief that it didn't occur to me they were totally devastated as well. This sort of thing didn't happen in their world either and they couldn't comprehend it. My brother later told me that Anne couldn't phone me earlier than she had because she couldn't stop crying long enough to speak. Each one was too distraught to ask me anything. That four-letter word was enough; they didn't need the details.

I remember looking at everyone and thinking how each person seemed different now. As I stared, I knew in my heart I must look different to them too. I felt like an alien. They were thinking things about me I had no control over. Everyone wanted to come in and have a look at the girl who was raped. Yeah, well, believe me, whatever you're imagining is fucking Disneyland compared to what's in my head, fucking Disneyland!

Mairead and I went upstairs to the chapel to say the rosary. The prayers I recited in school and prayers I said in Latin all came flooding back to me. Over and over we prayed, Mairead and I, until we could pray no more and cried together instead. She repeated how sorry she was that this had happened to me and I found her presence comforting. There is something calming and rhythmic in praying and it had a meditative effect on me that morning. The illusion was quickly shattered as the police interrupted to ask how I was. Before I could gather the energy to reply they told me Rachel had arrived. 'Oh, thank God for that!' It felt like I'd been waiting for hours for her to arrive but in reality it was probably only about twenty minutes. I knew the retching, crying, pacing, hair pulling and chain-smoking would resume once I left the room but at least I now had Rachel by my side. I ran outside, spotting her in the garden. I stopped and at the very sight of her lost it completely. 'Rachel, can you believe it?' I said. She hugged me for a long time, what felt like forever.

We drank tea, tea and more tea while I smoked around forty cigarettes in a row. I asked Phil to go to the shop as I needed deodorant and a toothbrush and he still wasn't allowed into the flat. It was then that the big guns arrived, a woman who looked like Helen Mirren in *Prime Suspect* in the nineties. She didn't introduce herself, just looked at me and left. She was more interested in the flat and her priority was the evidence the men in spacesuits who had just arrived could gather. My flat was a crime scene. A detective called John introduced himself in the garden, almost hidden amongst the fog of my cigarette smoke. He explained that he was leading the investigation and asked me questions about the robbery. When I said I had given him the pin numbers to my cards his face lit up and I couldn't help thinking it was almost like I'd handed him a Christmas present.

'He's already taken money out on my credit card,' I said. 'Wait – did they not tell you?' I feared Andrew or Lucy was in a spot of bother. Having met John and received assurances I would see him in due course, I was off to the Sapphire Unit to make my statement. The vomiting resumed leaving the house and walking past the flat to get into the police car.

I couldn't believe how many police were outside and the amount of yellow tape everywhere. Phil and Rachel's husband, David, left for the airport while Rachel and I went to the station. The Sapphire Unit had a separate entrance from the main police station, thank God. I'd never been in a police station before and I took that as a positive. We went into a small room with a sink and a kettle. Kettle or not, I wouldn't have had a cup of tea if it was offered; the room was disgustingly dirty and I didn't even want to sit down.

Giving a statement took what seemed like forever. I went through everything and Julie, the police woman, wrote it down. She couldn't possibly have written any slower. Rachel had to clean out the basin for me to be sick in, and verbalising the sequence of events brought on pooing which would continue for months to come. Can you imagine having diarrhoea in the police station? I couldn't even bring myself to be embarrassed about it. Turns out police officers really do sit, drink tea and have doughnuts. I'd always thought it was just on television but the officers laughed at me when I voiced my surprise. We were both offered food but declined and resumed our insistent tea drinking, even though I genuinely couldn't remember the last time I had eaten. I was pacing up and down, contemplating this fact, when I looked over at Rachel and realised she was crying. I stopped pacing and told Julie we had to take a break, that I had to speak to Rachel. I sat down beside her and softly asked, 'What's the matter? Are you okay?'

'I'm fine, Alana, it's just tough going listening to all this.'

'I know ... it's just complete madness.' I tried my best to soothe her. It hadn't occurred to me that it was hard for her to listen to what I was saying. Jesus, had I completely lost the plot already?

'Right!' I said. 'No more bloody tea, let's get this fucking madness finished.'

One statement later and we headed off to the Havens, a rape clinic. I was ignorant to the fact such places even existed and I dreaded the very thought of entering such a building, but I needn't have worried. Rachel was able to stay with me and the doctor and nurse who dealt with me were so sensitive. It felt like hundreds of swabs, evidence bags and the same questions repeatedly. 'Did he touch you here? What about here? Here?' they asked. The only part of me I could be certain He hadn't touched were the soles of my feet. And during the rape, He never touched my left breast. I know that because I didn't let Him. It was just one part of me I completely refused access to. I was trying so hard to be quiet that I kept one hand over my mouth. That hand was shaking so much that I used my other hand to hold my wrist to keep it there. My breast was between my arms with my elbow sort of resting on it. He tried to make me move my arm but I just wouldn't let go. *Fuck You. Not that one.* There's nothing special about it. It was just a matter of principle that was so important to me and it was a victory when He gave up and moved on.

The best part of the day was the shower. I must have spent an hour in there. It was clean and they gave me toiletries, fresh towels, clean clothes, a hairdryer and a toothbrush. My skin was raw from scrubbing and I still didn't feel clean. I felt dirty and ashamed and it still hadn't registered with me that what happened wasn't my fault. I walked out of the bathroom in a pair of tracksuit bottoms and an orange T-shirt. It wasn't my usual style but I was grateful and hardly in any position to complain. The doctor offered me the morning-after pill which I willingly accepted. Under no circumstances would I have His baby. I couldn't keep anything down, so the doctor gave me two pills, just in case. I took them both. We politely but firmly refused the offer of more food and even more tea – it seemed Rachel had no appetite either.

We were taken back to the police station and I was told I had to make a video statement. *They couldn't be serious?* I was brought into a room and Julie calmly sat down opposite me (Rachel wasn't allowed in this time). I sat with my back to the door and looked over my shoulder every other second in case someone came in and I couldn't see who it was. I had to go through every little detail again all the while being videoed. I managed to get through most of it, only becoming really hysterical at the end. I was just so tired. I needed a break. After more tea and copious cigarettes, I was ready to resume.

This time Julie asked me questions. I immediately noticed the tone of her voice was different: she was harsh and firm as she relentlessly asked me questions that we both knew she already knew the answer to. I was scared and didn't really understand what was going on. Just when I thought it couldn't get any worse then came the most repellent questions with crude words about orgasms, penises and vaginas. It was all so explicit and I wasn't used to speaking like that about such things. I felt totally betrayed by her. She was a completely different person. 'That's enough!' I said. 'I'm done here. I need to go home *now* and I can't do any more of this!' The retching, shaking and crying had started up again and my head felt like it was going to explode. Julie apologised and explained that she had to ask me these things so the defence wouldn't get a chance to shock me like she had. I stood my ground and told her she should have got someone else to ask me those questions or at least had the common decency to prepare me for what was coming. It was barbaric and there was no need for it. 'Now look what you've done,' I whispered as I continued to retch and shake. I was devastated.

Thankfully that seemed to be all the police needed that day. Unbelievably, it was eight o'clock and I was totally exhausted. Julie said she was going to drive us to Rachel's and my relief was palpable. Phil and David were still at the airport because Mum's flight had been delayed, and so we waited patiently in the car outside the house. And then they arrived: Mum, Paul, Phil and David. I wanted to wait in the car until they were in the house as I didn't want to be hysterical in the street, but stress and worry had obviously overtaken them because they paced up and down the street lighting cigarettes instead. 'Fuck it,' I said when I could wait no longer, 'we'll go now.' They were so late but really they arrived at exactly the right time.

Chapter Six

I got out of the car and tried to walk towards Paul but my legs just wouldn't do it.

He didn't see me at first. 'Paul! Paul!' He turned and a look of annoyance passed over his face.

'Fuck!' he said and flicked his cigarette to the ground, reaching me in seconds. I was hysterical, retching and shaking. I put my head on his shoulder and cried like I'd never cried before.

'Come on,' my mummy said, 'we'll go in.'

I suddenly realised we were all standing in the street crying, every single one of us. I didn't have the energy to put one foot in front of the other, so Paul half carried me inside and sat me down in a chair.

My memory of the next few days is a bit hazy. I assumed Julie, after she introduced herself, filled everyone in on what had happened because the questions stopped rather abruptly. We phoned my daddy, and my younger sister Maria wanted to talk to me desperately. She was the only one who was hysterically crying on the phone and, honestly, I was relieved to hear her so upset. Thank God someone recognised how bad it was and was as big of a mess as me. I was instantly comforted by her tears, which sounds strange but I could deal with it.

'I'm not sure I know what's going on at all,' I said. 'All I know is that I'll be home soon and then we'll see what happens.'

'Jesus,' Paul said, 'is she still crying?'

It wasn't what he said but the way he said it that made it so funny. He said she'd been crying all day.

'It's unbelievable,' he said with a look of astonishment on his face.

Paul filled me in on the phone call to our parents not long after I'd spoken with Maria. He told me he'd remained strong, didn't bow down or buckle under the pressure, and he'd made my father sit down before he spoke – no mean feat, let me tell you. My father's a formidable man and his word is usually gospel in our house. When my father tells you to do something, you do it with no questions asked. I'm super impressed with Paul and faintly amused that he's still in one piece and alive to tell the tale.

'Is she dead?' my mummy asked. 'Is she? Is she dead?' Paul told her, no, I wasn't dead but it wasn't good. She said that whatever it was was all right if I hadn't been murdered.

'Shut up, Teresa!' my daddy said.

Paul continued. It wasn't long into the conversation before the penny dropped with Mummy and she knew where it was headed. The penny didn't drop for Daddy.

'Paul, what the hell happened?' my daddy questioned.

Paul told them I was raped.

'What did you just say to me?' Daddy said. 'Don't you say a fucking thing like that to me, Paul. Don't you say that to me again.'

My daddy put his head in his hands and started to cry. He never even moved out of the chair and my mummy didn't say a word. Nothing, she said nothing at all. It's unheard of for her not to have an opinion about everything.

'Give me that phone,' she said and phoned Mairead's house in London.

I have four brothers and two sisters, and as the news travelled through the clan the drama unfolded. My younger sister, Maria, worked in a bank and was instructed to bring home money for Mum to bring with her to London. Maria arrived hysterically crying and when my daddy asked her where the money was she said she was so upset she forgot about it.

'You forgot the money?' my daddy said. 'How the fuck is your mother supposed to go to London with no money?'

Paul said Maria was asked very nicely, on numerous occasions, if she would stop crying but she couldn't do it.

'You wouldn't understand – she's my sister!' she reasoned.

'She's everyone's sister, Maria,' Paul said.

'But I'm a *girl!*' she wailed. I knew what she meant but I knew he probably wouldn't.

They phoned my youngest brother, Karl, who's eighteen, and told him there was an emergency with me and he'd be picked up from work only, amongst all the madness, they promptly forget about him. Karl wasn't collected and no one had the chance to tell him I was okay. He told me he thought I was dead, for three whole fucking hours he thought I was dead. During all the drama no one wanted to phone my sister Anne, for good reason. We shared a room in our youth, worked together and went out together. No one wanted to be the one to break the news to her but I was insistent I spoke to her.

They phoned her boyfriend first and asked him to pick her up from work. That's when Paul again shouldered the hideous burden of telling another person what had happened to me. I don't know what Paul said to Anne, but I do know she fell off her chair and her colleague had to take the phone and look after her until her boyfriend arrived. Paul told me Maria insisted on coming to the airport with them, nearly a two-hour drive, crying the whole way up the road. Snivelling in the back seat until Paul thought he was going to kill her.

'Stop it!' Paul said. 'I swear to God, I can't take it any more. Just stop it.'

Maria couldn't control herself, I was informed, and I was delighted, just absolutely delighted that someone else had cried all day too. Maria wanted to come to London but Mummy wouldn't let her. She had her son to look after and he was only four. Anne met them at the airport too and also wanted to come to London but my mother was adamant they were to stay at home. Both of them were too upset to fly over and this way they would have a day or two to collect themselves before I arrived.

The flight was delayed by three hours and my typically level-headed brother lost the plot at the information desk, telling the guy at the desk that he had a family emergency and couldn't wait another three hours for a flight to London. Paul called him a few choice names and threatened to flatten him when it was explained nothing could be done. Oh the drama just for a domestic flight from Belfast to London! It was ridiculous but it made me giggle. I was so glad to see them I never gave it a second thought that it took them so long to get to me. We chatted and drank tea and more tea until we went to bed, eventually dragging ourselves back downstairs again where we smoked cigarettes until Tuesday was finally over.

Phil came downstairs like a lunatic at five on Wednesday morning because he had just remembered he had seen Him behind the bin lorry outside the flat. He was distraught he hadn't remembered it before now, in all the madness. We would contact the police first thing and sent him back to bed to get some well-deserved sleep.

I was waiting for one of my friends to arrive from Leicester with some underwear. I didn't have any clothes and I didn't feel I could borrow underwear off Rachel – invading her home and dragging her into the wreckage seemed quite enough without asking her for a pair of pants too.

Julie and Sarah, the So-Ed officers, arrived shortly after nine to fingerprint me (and Phil for elimination purposes). Julie told us they had a suspect.

'What does that mean?' I asked.

'It means we think we know who we are looking for but we haven't found him yet,' she said. She couldn't really discuss it with me, however, as it would compromise the case.

'What case?' I asked.

'Your case. Your court case,' she said.

Court case. I hadn't thought about a court case, not even for a split second, never mind that I would have anything to do with it. I had never even been inside a courtroom. Fuck, I must have seemed so stupid. I went to the shower and stayed in it for a long time. No matter how hard I scrubbed I felt the same when I got out.

I was conscious of Rachel's rapidly rising stress levels and suggested she phone our friend Stephanie. The three of us and our partners regularly spent time together and always had a great laugh. Rachel, Stephanie and I were all senior staff nurses on the infectious diseases and the bone marrow transplant unit at a local children's hospital. We all worked together before I got my nurse specialist role and still made an effort to see each other. I thought Rachel could do with the support and Stephanie was en route as soon as she put the phone down.

Phil, David and Paul went to the flat to try and work out exactly what was missing. I hadn't a clue what else He'd taken but I needed my passport to get on the plane. Forensics were finished but I couldn't even think about going back there. The very thought of it made me cry, retch and shake once more. Phil's parents arrived soon after, along with Phil's sister and our lodger and friend, Emma, who had now suddenly become homeless too. Everyone was understandably upset. I don't think I made too much conversation except to reassure everyone again and again that I was fine.

Julie eventually said the police didn't need anything else from me and I could go home. Paul booked the flights for Thursday afternoon and everyone's mood instantly lifted. I was so looking forward to going home that I couldn't think or talk about anything else – I couldn't wait to see everyone and get into my own bed. Maybe I could even sleep.

Stephanie arrived like a breath of fresh air. She is honest, funny, kind and sensitive – just exactly the sort of person you need in a crisis, and my mummy instantly warmed to her. She took Rachel for a walk and they went to get buns and doughnuts for all the coppers at the station who were working hard to find the suspect. They bought groceries and poor David made even more food which nobody really ate much of, preferring more tea and a ridiculous number of cigarettes.

Thankfully, however, we had now moved ourselves outside to enjoy the lovely sunny day and at least the house became somewhat smoke-free. Stephanie's partner, Eric, arrived too and the house became a hub of activity. At some point everyone settled down for the night and Mum and I sat outside. There was no point in trying to lie down, I just couldn't do it and knew I would get no sleep. God love her, she must have been exhausted but she sat up with me anyway drinking tea and smoking the night away. Roll on tomorrow.

Thursday morning finally arrived and we got ready to go. This was relatively easy for me as I had nothing to bring home anyway – not even my mind, which had already started to wander off into the unknown. The shaking continued as did the pooing and I still couldn't eat a bite. The morning brought fresh news: the police had found their suspect and arrested him on suspicion of burglary. This brought whoops of delight from everyone in the house, everyone but me. I was terrified. The knot in my stomach intensified with the news and I didn't get the relief everyone was expecting. What if it was the wrong man? The police seemed fairly sure but couldn't tell me why or how they were so confident. Again, it would compromise the case – another punch for Julie was on the cards. My mother was hoping for two charges to be brought against him: rape and burglary, but I didn't give a hoot about the charges. I just wanted to go home. The phone call soon came from the main man himself, Detective

Inspector Whatever, advising me of a change of plan: I couldn't go home after all. They wanted me to go to the police station to identify Him in a line-up. Un-*fucking*-believable!

'I can't do that,' I told him. 'You may remember that I was blindfolded for most of it and I only got a quick look at Him when I was half asleep. What if I don't pick Him out and He gets away with it?' An image of Him popped into my head and I almost vomited. 'Oh, no,' I said. 'I don't think I could cope with doing that. I really don't want to do it. I really don't want to do that.'

John explained how important for the case it was for me to identify Him. They had brought Him in for questioning but didn't have enough evidence to charge Him unless they could specifically place Him in my flat at the time of the burglary. He told me the suspect was very clever regarding to the law and He knew they couldn't charge Him. He was saying nothing and He knew they were going to have to release Him.

'We really need you to do it. He won't see you but He'll know you're there. There will be six people of a similar height and stature. Each person will step forward, say something and then step back. Once they're all finished, you call out the number of the man you think it is. Do you think you could do that?' he enquired.

'No, I don't think I could do that at all,' I said. 'I really don't think I could do it.'

My voice was shaking and I was crying with the sheer panic and terror at having to be in such proximity to Him. It was just too much. John said he would leave me to think about it and talk it over with my family. We had some time before they had to interview Him again and I could let him know my decision when I was ready. I was so confused. Didn't I just say I didn't want to do it? Didn't he understand 'no'? Did I have a choice at all? And when was I going to be allowed to go home?

I went outside to tell the troops the news – Rachel and David's house was so crowded we had taken to sitting outside. Mummy was of the impression I would have to do it, that He couldn't get away with it. I roared and shouted at her that I just wanted to go home. 'You can do it, Alana,' she tried to assure me.

My brother and Phil took me into the living room and tried to talk rationally to me. It had obviously been decided that I couldn't be trusted to have a rational, logical discussion with the police, and in future someone else was to speak to them on my behalf and relay the information to me. So, with extreme reluctance on my part, we phoned them back and told them I would do it.

I then remembered that His phone had rang, His mobile rang when He was in my bedroom, and at the time I had thought maybe someone was waiting for Him outside. Paul thought this an important piece of information and rang John back to tell him. He played me different ringtones until I got the right one. This was important apparently, although I couldn't understand why.

So we waited for the call for Julie to take me to the station. But a couple of hours later further developments meant I was no longer required to do the line-up. What did that mean? *What was going on?* He had admitted to burgling my flat on Tuesday morning but denied rape. It was now up to The Crown Prosecution to decide what to charge Him with. *The crown who?* I was lost as to the meaning of it all. Why the sudden change of heart? Why go from saying nothing to admitting to being there? Oh, well, of course they weren't at liberty to say … that may compromise the case. The frustration was overwhelming.

Two charges, my mum said over and over. She wanted two charges. I just wanted to go home. *Is anybody listening to me? I just want to go home. And we missed the goddam plane.*

Chapter Seven

The Helen Mirren lookalike phoned me a few hours later to impart the good news: He had been charged with burglary and rape. She said this was very good news, that I should celebrate and have a glass of wine. They were having one. Oh God, no, I told myself, if I start drinking now I'll never stop – I was with the programme enough to know that.

The troops were waiting for the news but they had to wait until I'd finished puking and hyperventilating enough to talk. Finally, the flights were rebooked for Friday morning. Phil and my brother went for a drink and we phoned home with the news. My mummy was simply delighted. There would be a trial, they said, maybe in six months or a year. A year. A year of my life. I had to give Him a whole year of my life before I could begin to put this terrible thing behind me. Well, I'd give Him that year and hope to God He never took a year off anyone else.

Another night of no sleep and we went to the airport. It was excruciating saying goodbye to everyone, especially Rachel who had been like my right leg for three days. I was distraught at leaving her. Once through security we got a coffee and made our way to the smoking area. A black man sat down beside me. I dropped my coffee on the floor and stood up. He stood up too, obviously startled at my reaction.

'Are you all right?' he asked.

'Oh God, please don't touch me,' I said. 'I'm so sorry.'

He terrified me and it wasn't in the slightest his fault. I went to the bathroom and broke down. I was disgusted at myself for my reaction towards him just because of the colour of his skin, but I couldn't help it. This time the tears were of helplessness and sadness. Had I turned into a terribly shallow person as well as everything else? Was I going to judge people on their skin colour? I hoped with all my heart that would pass with time. I didn't want to tar every man with the same brush as that wanker.

Then we were in the air and nobody spoke a word. The tiredness had finally got to Mummy and it was obvious she too couldn't wait to get home. The relief when we landed and I saw the 'Welcome to Belfast' sign almost made me poo myself but I made it to the toilet in the nick of time. My two sisters were waiting for me when we came through security. We stood there crying and hugging for a long time.

Daddy was parking the car, and when we met him out the front, right outside the airport door, the tears returned. None of us cared though. 'Oh, hello, Daddy,' I said. We cried all the harder then. Anne's boyfriend was driving too, so the boys went with him and I sat in the middle of my two sisters on the way home. By the time we pulled into the driveway my legs were shaking so much I could hardly get out of the car and into the house. I resisted the urge to give thanks on my knees in the driveway, but only just.

I was persuaded to go to bed, and I slept for four hours, an impressive feat by my standards. It was the first time I had rested since Monday and it was now Friday afternoon. Every time someone came to check on me I jumped up, terrified, in the bed. My sisters went into town to get me a few things: pants, socks, pyjamas, clothes and toiletries. My brothers came round one by one that evening. It brought even more crying and hugging and continually telling everyone I was fine. I overheard my mother on the phone telling her sister I was in 'bad shape'. *Bad shape?* Didn't even begin to cover it.

Victim Support came on Monday, a wee woman called Maud who was about seventy with bluish hair. I liked her instantly but I wasn't ready to talk to anyone – I could barely get a sentence out without crying. It was almost Tuesday again and I had no idea how I was going to get through the day, never mind tomorrow.

My friends all gradually called in too, each bringing gifts or something I would need. Each one so upset and so shocked. I had spoken to most of them on the telephone on The Terrible Tuesday. We'd been friends since playschool – the chicks, the gang, the rat pack, as some liked to call us. You never get one but you got all of us. We'd been friends for twenty-five years despite all the dramas, teenage angst and boyfriend swapping. Of course, sometimes we hated each other but it was never for too long and certainly never for real. I'd shared some of the best days of my life with these girls and now I was sharing the worst day too. They would be there for me, of that I was sure. It was so comforting, so familiar, I almost felt relaxed. We sat out the back of my parents' house, drank wine and let the shock wear off. We talked crap like we normally did – of course they would accept me even if I was broken, hysterical and vacant in the head. With them I didn't have to pretend I was okay. They told me I would get through it with their support, and I truly wanted to believe them.

My English friends, Rachel and David and Stephanie and Eric, came to visit on separate weekends. They stayed at my parents' house for a week. It felt like my father was continually at the airport dropping off or picking up one of my friends, and my parents treated every one of them like gold dust, so grateful were they for their generous help and support to me. Their short appearances broke the month of July up nicely, and with the warm weather we spent most of their visits outside. Between family and friends we somehow managed to muddle through the days while Mummy sat with me through the nights until it was time for my first appointment.

Now, after the build-up to it, my first appointment was over and done with and I was surprised by the relief I felt. The relief at having shared every awful bit of it and still being in one piece was almost euphoric. It was excruciating sharing it all but it didn't kill me. I thought if I could do it once, then maybe, more importantly, I could do it again at the trial. Judy and I had an instant bond through sharing my worst day, and I felt like she understood; Judy got it, the awfulness of it, what it had done to my insides, my head and my life. I was so relieved she got it and so relieved that she had a plan to get us through it all because, honestly, I'd nothing.

———~∽∾◦◦∾∽~———

I settled into a routine of awfulness, of continual exhaustion and perpetual anxiety. I was scared of everything that moved and every noise the house made even though I'd spent my life in it. It was extremely stressful to overcome the challenges of daily living: eating, sleeping, washing and even talking was a test. I found it so difficult to hold a reasonable conversation with people without wandering off somewhere in my head. My family and friends found the change in me very difficult to deal with. I was so talkative and bubbly before The Terrible Tuesday, but most days since I could hardly muster the energy to speak let alone entertain anyone. Other days I was so irrationally angry I was sure if I spoke I would end up killing someone. It wasn't fair on anyone, so I decided to do something about it. I planned to try and do something difficult every day.

The first thing was going to the shop by myself: leave the house, walk around the corner, go up the hill, open the door, walk in, buy something and walk down the hill again, which all sounded reasonable enough. However, on my first attempt I had a panic attack simply going up the hill and had to sit on a wall for a while. I continued on, but once I was in the shop I couldn't even remember what I was supposed to buy, so I just walked around the shop aimlessly hoping it would come to me. It didn't. My daddy suddenly poked his head round one of the aisles, 'Are you all right? You're taking an awfully long time.'

'Oh, Daddy, I can't remember what I came in for.' I was almost crying in the aisle.

'Come on,' he said, and took me down the hill in the car. 'Sure, it doesn't matter, you can try again tomorrow.'

It was baffling. I lived in London, got a bus then the tube to work and managed to blend in with millions of people. Now I couldn't even go to the local shop without having some sort of breakdown. What sort of a basket case had I turned into? What a nightmare. But I stuck at it and went every day until I no longer panicked at not being within shouting distance of my parents or the possibility of meeting someone I had to talk to while I was there. After a while I even started to walk to my appointments but always ended up arriving super anxious and exhausted from being hyper vigilant and terrified on my long journey there. 'Don't push yourself too hard,' Judy said. 'Can you trust that these things will improve in time? Can you try to do that?' I could certainly try but I couldn't see how it would help me now, which was all I was capable of focusing on.

My new focus arrived shortly after. My brother, Peter, came one night proclaiming there was something for me in the back of his car. I went outside and opened the passenger door to the cutest brown Labrador puppy curled up on the seat staring back at me. Peter carefully lifted him up and placed him on the ground. He walked over to me and immediately vomited at my feet. Nice to meet you too. We convinced ourselves it was due to the car journey, but it wasn't. He continued to retch and couldn't keep any food down. I named him Charlie Brown and he was the best present I'd ever received. I was consumed with worry that I was somehow transmitting the shaking, retching and puking to Charlie Brown and this made me try even harder to stop. We left the pup at the vet's, who must have thought I was nuts when I told him I was in a very bad place and couldn't cope if anything happened to the dog, so could he please try and find out what was wrong with him. The vet wanted to know where we got him and his date of birth. With this information he was able to find out that one of Charlie Brown's siblings had recently died of lungworm. The vet hadn't seen it in twenty years because it was simple to worm the mother during pregnancy and the pups would be fine. It was touch-and-go for poor innocent Charlie Brown who had to go to the vets every week for injections. I made him soup and sat up with him every night. His food was eighty bucks a bag but I didn't give a shit as long as he didn't die. Everyone knew I would have a complete breakdown if anything happened to the bloody dog.

Judy told me that continually being fearful and anxious used all the energy you had. Not only that but everything in reserve as well, which is why my nerves were completely frazzled and I felt constantly on the edge. She told me not to give power to the thought that the dog might die. She told me that when I thought about Charlie Brown dying I had to follow it through to a positive outcome in my head. From then on I found comfort in talking to Charlie Brown, telling him he wasn't allowed to be sick because I needed him, telling him about the walks on the beach we would have together once I learned to drive.

Slowly but surely Charlie Brown's health improved. With this new-found lease of life it became apparent he was a bit of a nutjob. Nothing wrong with that. I was a bit of a nutjob myself. We were well-suited. He gave me great focus and a purpose for each day. He needed out, fed, walked and brushed. The shit needed lifted and the yard needed hosed down. He was extremely gentle yet a fierce guard dog at the same time. He gave me confidence to go out walking and be in the house by myself. He slept at the door of my room and I knew anyone would have a hard job getting past him. I started to sleep for four hours a night. It doesn't sound like much but it was a great improvement on nothing.

The only downside of finally sleeping was the horrendous nightmares. Every night, the same thing over and over again, some awful part of The

Terrible Tuesday. At first it was the noise of his footsteps in the hall and him opening the door. I woke hyperventilating, panicking and crying and I was so glad of Charlie Brown in the room with me. I slept with the light on and the door slightly open. I asked Judy why those dreams kept reoccurring. Apparently it was my mind's way of making me deal with it. Judy said once I dispelled the energy surrounding that specific part of it I wouldn't dream of it any more. It was fascinating. It was like my mind and body were trying to protect me from a complete breakdown, only letting me deal with one part at a time. Who knows, maybe my mind was cleverer than I gave it credit for. It knew that those small moments were all I could cope with for the time being.

Every night when my daddy walked down the hall to go to bed, I'd panic and call out, 'Is that you, Dad?', because I heard the footsteps and saw someone else in my head. My mind would race and I'd watch the door like a maniac in case it opened and He was there. It was ridiculous – I knew it was my dad, yet I'd ask every night. He'd quietly answer 'Yes, it's me,' until one day Mummy asked me very nicely to try and stop asking Dad the same question every night – he found it upsetting before bed. I would try, I told her, but I couldn't guarantee the question wouldn't come out of my mouth again. There was no point in making promises I just couldn't keep.

Chapter Eight

My poor parents. They must never have got a wink of sleep or knew what to expect from me from one day to the next. One morning they innocently decided to take a trip into town, and considering I didn't get much rest they didn't wake me to say they were leaving the house. I woke up to someone knocking the bedroom window. I was paralysed with fear until I heard my neighbour calling, telling me not to worry, that it was the window cleaners. I called after her but she was already down the path, so I jumped out of bed and grabbed my phone. I went to run out the patio doors in my parents' bedroom but a window cleaner was already there going about his work. I screamed. Before he could even turn to look at me I ran up the hall in the direction of the front door. The other cleaner was in the dining room. I screamed even louder, scrambled out the front door and stood in the garden in the pissing rain in only pyjama shorts and a vest top weeping.

That was the moment I'd been waiting for: I punched my father's number into my phone and he answered almost immediately. 'Where *are* you?' I screamed. 'There are two men in the house cleaning the fucking windows. What the fuck is going on? WHERE ARE YOU?' My dad, obviously shocked by my sudden outburst, asked in a panicky voice where I was. 'I'm in the fucking garden, in my pyjamas, in the rain!'

Before he could hang up I heard Mum say, 'Jesus Christ'. That said it all.

It was probably the first time they had left me alone in the house since The Terrible Tuesday. Who could have predicted our neighbour would let the window cleaners in and think nothing of it? Who could have known that it would throw me over the edge and hurtle me into survival mode?

I planned an escape route as I waited. I was positioned exactly between the house and the garden wall, so if either of them came to the front door I would easily have made it to the wall before they made it to me. I pulled my hair, shook and tried not to vomit when my parents pulled up. They walked into the house, Dad explaining to the window cleaners that I was in the throes of a nervous breakdown in the garden. Mum, meanwhile, opened the kitchen window and shouted, 'Do you want a cup of tea?' What else could she say? I couldn't breathe and was about to pass out. I must have been the colour of a corpse. 'We should have told you we were going to Homebase,' she said.

And I was back to square one. Back to the shaking and retching and puking and jumping every single time someone walked in the door. More worryingly, though, I was back to the vacant place in my head.

It was around this time one of my friends ended up being off work. She was a bit of a wreck too, although she kept it well hidden, and we settled into a pattern of walking and swimming every day. It made a nice change to shower at the pool and involved both things I cared about at the same time: exercising and washing. Swimming had a very calming effect on my insides – the only thing I could concentrate on was breathing at the right time, so there was no room in my head for anything more sinister. Most of the time I swam until I no longer had the energy to hold the knot in my stomach. I would reluctantly leave the pool with barely the energy to walk to the changing room. I had no problem getting changed or getting into the pool – I suppose because I had my friend at my side and was never alone. I also had no idea how I looked in a swimsuit, nor did I care, and I'm sure that played its part too.

Everyone treated me like broken glass at the beginning and tried their hardest to walk around me. I couldn't blame them – they were constantly walking on eggshells in my presence so short was my temper and so crazy were my mood swings. Everyone, that is, except Paul. Instead he bought me a ticket to New York. He works for the Irish government and was to be based in New York for three months. *A ticket to New York* – was he mad? I could hardly go to the shop without having a breakdown and he wanted me to get on a plane by myself and go to New York? My parents broke the happy news of my upcoming adventure, and instead of joy and gratitude I almost lost my head altogether. They were adamant: I had to go.

'He can't get a refund, so you'll just have to go,' my mother told me sternly.

'Fuck New York,' I told them, and off I went.

———∿∿⌒⌒⌒∿∿———

In hindsight, it was a ridiculous idea. Panic attacks overcame me at the airport and on the plane. I stood outside the airport in New York for over an hour incapable of getting into a taxi. To my dismay, all the taxi drivers were black. I eventually encountered an Egyptian taxi driver who had vitiligo. That eased my sense of fear because I couldn't truly be sure what colour he was. He dropped me at the hotel and I made my way up to my brother's apartment. Paul was at work and I thought a shower would calm me down and settle me into my holiday. Maybe then I could even go for a walk. I was already in the shower when someone walked into the bathroom. I screamed and opened the shower door. It was the cleaner apologising profusely in broken English, 'I sorry, I sorry, Madam. I come back later and clean.' I couldn't make a sound, and when she left I slid down the wall and sat on the floor. How could I be this unlucky? Did this sort of thing happen to people all the time or did the entire universe and everyone in it just hate me? After the retching and shaking eased off I got out of the shower and poured a large glass of wine, pairing it with a couple of diazepam the doctor had given me. I could do nothing but sit and wait for Paul to come back from work. Unsurprisingly, the combination of booze and pills took the edge off, and by the time Paul got back I was laughing hysterically at what had happened. What a sight the cleaner must have seen!

On the way home I felt exhilarated and proud that I had, even in my extremely fucked-up state, managed a trip to America. Not only that, I even managed to enjoy myself. I couldn't wait to get back and tell Judy about the cleaner coming into the bathroom. I was so looking forward to my next appointment it shocked me. It was the longest I'd gone without therapy and I felt like a pressure valve was going to blow in my head if I didn't get to speak to Judy soon. Would it have been ridiculous to telephone her from the hotel? Would it have crossed the line – the professional boundary I knew all too well? Did I care? I didn't care about the line but I had managed to restrain myself from making the call

'Who do you think you were talking to in the bathroom of your flat?' Judy asked me when I filled her in on all the gory details of my trip. She had a habit of doing that, bringing me right back down to earth with a bang all in one single question, and now I was right back there in the bathroom.

'I have no idea,' I told her.

'*Really?*' she said. 'No idea at all?'

'Well,' I said, 'I used to see things in my bedroom at night, usually when I was saying my prayers – since I was small. When I was young they scared me a lot and I wet the bed, but as I got older they didn't scare me as much even though I still didn't understand what was going on. Usually it began with a funny feeling coming over my entire body – pins and needles everywhere, my limbs suddenly heavy and I was unable to move. It was like my body was paralysed. I would feel someone hugging me, whispering in my ear, or I would see someone at the end of the bed. They always said the same thing: "Everything will be all right. Everything will be all right." Other nights I woke to someone sitting on the bed. After I sat up they would tell me everything would be okay. A youngish looking guy, who said his name was Keith, appeared quite often, always wearing a shirt and tie, and I asked him what he was doing. He said he was just reminding me I could see him and telling me I would be okay. Sometimes I woke to see a darkness above my head moving around the room that would follow me down the hall when I built up the courage to hightail it to my parents' bed.' I looked up at her suddenly, 'Not once, ever, did my mother make me go back to my own bed. I told her I had a bad dream and she let me sleep between them. That went on until I was about thirteen, then one day Dad said it wasn't right, that I was too old to be in their bed, so I hopped into my sister's bed instead.'

'Did you tell anyone about it?' Judy asked.

'Oh, yes, I told Mum about it all the time.'

My mother had taken the whole thing very seriously. She had the house blessed and we went to Mass a lot. She even took me to see a couple of priests. One said it was perfectly natural, normal and reassuring to receive a message from the other side and that he often felt the presence of his mother since she had passed away. My mum wasn't happy with that having had an old-school, traditional Roman Catholic upbringing. She was brought up to believe that people who can see or communicate with the other side must get it from the devil, and so we saw another priest who said I had these experiences because of sins I hadn't yet committed – sex before marriage, masturbation or breaking my pledge by drinking alcohol before I was eighteen. I found it completely ridiculous. Then I went to the same centre I saw Judy in and met with the two wonderful women who ran it. When I explained the experiences to them, they didn't think it was much of a problem and wanted me to meet with a psychic. My mother refused as the psychic had been excommunicated from the Catholic Church. Game over! Mum and I didn't talk about it too much after that and eventually I stopped telling her altogether. Despite the priest's take on it, the experiences continued well into my twenties, even throughout my move to Leicester and then London. The only thing that changed was I stopped praying at night when I got into bed and went to sleep with lights and music on so I wouldn't be disturbed.

It was weird because during the attack in my bedroom I felt totally alone – like His presence filled the room and there wasn't room for anything else. It was different in the bathroom, though. I felt like someone was with me. I didn't know who it was but I felt the presence of someone, so much so that when I asked for help I got it. I knew they helped me get out alive, they showed me the way and spurred me on to open the door. It sounded strange, I knew, but it was the truth. I was comforted that Judy didn't think I was mad as a child, nor did she think I was mad now. Genuinely, there was nothing I could say that would phase her. She didn't seem surprised by my admission of spooky visions, and suggested that maybe my nightly visitations were a spirit guide or guardian. It sounded a bit weird but not impossible. If there was one thing I knew for sure, it's that anything' was possible.

Judy asked if I'd heard of shamanism. I hadn't, so she explained it was part of the work at the centre. They used shamanic journeying as a tool to help the healing process. She explained that in shamanic terms life was a journey. We were spiritual beings made of energy and connected by energy, and each of us was on a physical journey. Shamanism theorised that there were three worlds: the one we lived in was the middle world; the lower world was where we met animal and spirit guides who assisted us on our journey in this lifetime; and the upper world was where the spirits resided in what we commonly called heaven – which all sounded a bit *Alice in Wonderland* even for me. Judy said that we journeyed to the other worlds to ask for guidance and assistance from our power animals and guides but we needed a method of getting there. She gave examples such as climbing down through the roots of a tree and walking through a tunnel or cave. I stopped her there.

'Jesus, it sounds totally crazy! Are you one of those weird people?' I said.

She laughed. 'I'm afraid so, but don't worry. You're one of those weird people too.'

Touché. If I wasn't weird before The Terrible Tuesday, I certainly was now. I wanted to be open to everything Judy suggested, so I tried my first shamanic journey to meet my power animal ... and nothing happened. It was a simple process: I lay down, relaxed and covered my eyes (a difficult thing for me because I was super anxious about not being able to see, which rendered me completely unable to even remotely relax). I listened to a drumbeat that was supposed to alter my state of consciousness and allow me to enter the shamanic state. I, meanwhile, was listening to the drumbeat through headphones and worrying about not being able to hear anything else but the drums. The combination of not being able to see and hear took my anxiety levels to fever pitch. I knew I could trust Judy to watch over me but it was still extremely difficult to concentrate.

My first few attempts resulted in lots of lights, like circles in front of my eyes, but nothing much else. It was after my third attempt that I had a different answer for her. I told her she would think I'd lost my mind but I continued: I went through a hole in a tree and down a tunnel that opened into a clearing. I met a cat at the bottom of the tunnel, a very large one. We were in a forest area and danced around a fire together. It was so real in my mind that I found no reasoning for it other than I'd actually gone a bit mad. I expected Judy to agree but instead she said, 'Oh, good! You've made contact and now we can get started.' Oh shit, now we'd both lost the plot.

Shamanism drew me in rather quickly after that first experience, and I researched a bit when I got home. My understanding was that it was a spiritual practice to assist everyday living. Although 'shaman' was a Siberian word, shamanism had been practised the world over for thousands of years. A shaman, or shamanic practitioner, interacted directly with spirits by journeying to the three worlds addressing the spiritual aspects of illness, performing soul retrievals, divine information and helping the spirits of the deceased crossover. Shamanism believed that everything that existed was alive, had a spirit and had an energy, all of which were joined with the earth and its life forces. It was a method of healing described as a journey of deep personal and spiritual growth.

Initiation usually began with a deep trauma, when you realised you were a bit screwed on the inside and needed to look inward to sort it out. You were taken back to your spiritual bones, as such, and through shamanic work you gradually built yourself up and began a gradual healing process aided by power animals from the lower world and spirit guides or helpers from all three worlds.

It made great sense to me. I was aware I'd been stripped of everything I possessed mentally, physically, emotionally and materially – never mind spiritually, and was unsure as to what was important any more. I was lost as to the direction my life was going to take or how it might turn out. I felt I'd lost something inside myself I never even knew I had. How could I find it again and become normal? In shamanic terms this was described as 'soul loss'. During a deep trauma parts of the soul broke away from the psyche to protect the person from complete breakdown. Of course I didn't know this when I started journeying, and I had asked Judy not to tell me what was supposed to happen so I wouldn't worry about getting it wrong – I was willing to try anything to speed my recovery but didn't want to spook myself with all the details. So I didn't know what to expect, nor did I realise the significance of my journeys and how they would allow me to move forward. I thought of them in the same way I thought of everything in my life: in a remote, detached manner that made little sense at the time.

Chapter Nine

We began some spiritual work which was extremely frustrating as it limited the time I had to complain about the challenges of everyday life and how vexing it had all become. I was incensed by the lack of information on the trial which was scheduled to start on 14 January. Any information I asked for was politely refused because it might compromise the case – it drove me mad with anger that everything seemed to work in His favour. I wasn't allowed to know if He had any previous convictions or if He was a class A drug user. Nothing. I was given no option but to wait for the results of the GUM clinic tests to find out if He'd given me a sexually transmitted disease on top of everything else. It all seemed unnaturally cruel and impossibly unfair.

Judy and I journeyed and asked for help in dealing with my anger and my other emotions which were so out of sync with each other. At any given time fear, frustration, helplessness or panic would overtake me completely and uncontrollably. The overwhelming panic that I would never feel right or normal again, that I would be left in this vacant state of nothingness for eternity was too much to bear. Despite that, I was getting better at shamanism and was finding it easier to journey to the other worlds without dwelling on the absurdity of it all. I often met Keith in the upper world, and I felt my batteries recharge as we lay in the sun together. I met deceased members of my family who came for a friendly chat and a hug. It left me with a firm belief not only the existence of heaven but that heaven was a place of incredible light and love. I had first-hand experience of darkness, so it was nice to spend time at the other end of the scale.

The police visited my home town, going over my statement and making final adjustments before the trial began. My mother tried her hardest to accommodate them despite me chain-smoking all over their apple pie and numerous cups of tea. It was then I remembered I'd forgotten to tell them he had taken me through the flat looking for my laptop, refusing to believe I didn't own one. They suggested we watched the video statement as it needed transcribing, and while doing so I could point out any mistakes or anything else I'd left out. The video evidence had yet to be admitted into court and I was incensed I had had to do it in the first place if it was going to be inadmissible anyway. 'Well, there's a first time for everything!' Julie said. Poor Julie, I wanted to punch her again. We discussed where I would feel most comfortable viewing the tape and quickly decided it should be at the centre with Judy. Her support might be needed in case I found watching it traumatic. Understatement of the century perhaps?

The shaking started as soon as Julie pressed play, and I could taste the vomit at the back of my throat. The extreme physical symptoms were incredible given that I went to a completely vacant place in my head at the same time. 'Your body remembers it,' Judy told me. I knew she was right. It must have been helpful for her to see the video, it was a true snapshot of me that day, even though I had shared every detail of The Terrible Tuesday with her. It can't have been easy watching for her though, and the longer it went on the more difficult it was for everyone. Judy was quite protective of her charges, and when Julie started asking me disgusting questions I imagined she might have wanted to punch Julie herself, not that she would ever have shown it.

The police asked how I felt about giving evidence in court. Strangely, once I got my head around there being a court case, I never felt I wouldn't be able to give evidence – there was a firm belief in my mind that I had to do it, and it wasn't a rash decision I could choose to back out of at the final hour either. It wasn't just because it might stop Him doing it to someone else, although that held great significance for me. It was because it was wrong. What He did was wrong. Wrong and even worse that He did it to me in my own bed in my own house. It was unacceptable. Another reason was because I was telling the truth: every word of my statement was the absolute truth – I had nothing to hide. On the rare days I was feeling brave and full of anger, I realised I'd nothing to be ashamed of and I refused to feel shame for something I didn't do.

On other days I was too terrified to contemplate being in the same room as Him. I hadn't given much thought to the practicalities of it all but the police said I could travel to London to look round the courtroom before the trial began. After some discussion it was decided that forewarned is forearmed, as they say, and preparation was the key. I might never have seen the inside of a courtroom before but I was damn sure He had and I didn't want Him having any advantage over me, never mind at the get-go. A solicitor friend assured me this would most definitely not be his first offence; he was too careful and showed knowledge of forensics which suggested he might have done something similar before. That disgusted me and it joined the list of things I refused to think about.

After the police arranged the courtroom visit, Phil and I eagerly went to look at where the trial would take place. We were met by two lovely girls from Victim Support who showed us round and carefully explained the procedure for giving evidence. Phil would be called to testify along with myself and Mairead, and that was the sum of information we had about the scheduling of the trial. The first thing that surprised and seriously worried me was just how small the room was – how physically close my father and I had to be to Him. It was so much smaller than it looked on television. He would be kept behind a clear plastic wall but it couldn't have been more than a few feet from where my family and I would sit.

The Victim Support girls advised me I could have a screen put up to shield me from Him while I was giving evidence, but they needed to know in advance if I wanted it so it could be organised in time. 'No,' I said defiantly, 'you might not understand but I'll never give Him the impression I'm scared of Him. Never again will He think He has any control over me in any way.' When we met it would be on an equal footing. I'd done nothing wrong and I wouldn't hide behind a screen. He would see me and I would see Him. I would face Him with as much dignity and courage as I could muster. It surprised even me how strongly I felt about it but standing in the empty courtroom made it suddenly so real. It was only a couple of months away and I was still a complete wreck, mentally and physically. How was I ever going to manage it?

The details of the trial consumed me. I was unable to sleep and eat; the very prospect of being in that room with Him. When I arrived home I scheduled extra appointments with Judy so we could continue with my shamanic work and also take time to prepare for the trial. I had never divulged the intimate details of The Terrible Tuesday with my family or friends, nor had anyone asked to know, so the thought of my parents, especially my father, having to listen to the details petrified me to my core. The thought of sharing that information with twelve complete strangers seemed an equally impossible task. I was afraid of crying in front of everyone – especially Him. I was afraid they wouldn't believe me and it would all be for nothing. I was afraid of getting it wrong, of recollecting some small, insignificant detail wrong and the defence crucifying me. It happened on television and it was extremely unpleasant to say the least. Perhaps most of all, I was afraid I wouldn't recognise Him or that it would be the wrong man. I was genuinely afraid of everything to do with it.

———— ഗ്രൂഗ്രൂഗ്രൂ ————

We discussed my pent-up fear at my first appointment after my London visit. Judy told me that everyone had different coping mechanisms and dealt with fear in their own way. She also said that everyone would cope with the trial because they had no choice. She reminded me that a lot of woman didn't get this far and wouldn't contemplate giving evidence in court. I was reminded of my undergrad placement working with inpatients in a mental health facility: so many vacant-looking women with Brillo-pad hair spending their day drinking tea, chain-smoking in their pyjamas and not saying very much. A routine I now knew all too well. These women had stories as terrible as mine which drove them to such a facility; stories they simply couldn't move past. I understood that feeling, I really did, but if I didn't try and move past it I would be stuck in the awfulness of it forever. I had to see this through to its legal conclusion before I could attempt some semblance of a normal life.

'Do you think He's going to give evidence?' I asked Judy. She did. How else could He refute my version if He didn't give evidence himself? I hadn't thought of it like that. I had to hear his voice again. A disgusting notion. Maybe it was a good thing I knew nothing about the trial after all. Maybe the details would push me over the edge and I wouldn't be able to see the whole thing through.

'Do you know his name?' Judy asked me. *His name.* As if He was a person – the same as her or me, with a name, an address and a next of kin. 'No, no, I don't want to know his name. I don't want to know anything about Him,' I told her. I knew far too much about Him already:

He was tall and overweight, street-smart and poorly educated. He was a criminal, a burglar, a rapist. He was violent and controlling, had little regard for human life, with darkness inside Him instead of light. I knew I was nothing like Him. I knew I had never encountered anyone like Him before and hoped never to do so again. I already knew enough about Him to last me a lifetime.

———⁓⁓⁓⁓———

The police were confident we were ready for trial, and the only thing left was for me to meet the barrister who had agreed to take the case. Apparently it wasn't easy to win a rape case, something I was blissfully unaware of before. Unsurprisingly, barristers disliked tricky-to-prove cases as they had less chance at winning. Fair enough. Most people would rather be successful at what they do for a living, me included. I strove to be an excellent nurse, a constant work in progress.

The barrister was a woman, which I was eternally grateful for, and I instantly felt comfortable in her presence despite her posh voice. She said that Phil would be called first, me second, and that it would take most of Monday and Tuesday for me to give my evidence. I was instantly terrified and felt under pressure – two days on the stand. I couldn't allow myself to think about it, not for a second, and as soon as I did I pushed it away. Mairead was to be called next and then a forensic pathologist. They usually dealt with dead people but he was a specialist in bruising and apparently my body's bruising was consistent with my story. When my bruises had come out, we had phoned John and he had sent a medical photographer to my parents' house to take photos. The photographer asked for the chair in the living room to be moved and for me to stand against the wall. I tried not to vomit being in such proximity to a strange man even with Mum present. Unsurprisingly, I wouldn't let her leave the room long enough to make him a cup of tea.

The doctor from the Havens was to be the final witness to give evidence on our side. Then it was up to the defence to present their case and we would see if He took the stand. The barrister thought He would give evidence – she sincerely hoped He would and looked forward to cross-examining Him. I was in awe of the balls she had – there wasn't a sliver of fear in sight, but then she didn't know Him the way I did and wasn't afraid. The trial was to take the full week and the barrister hoped to have a verdict by Friday afternoon. I felt twelve years old, and that she was speaking in a different language at times. Most of it was beyond me and my brain couldn't focus. She said I wouldn't be back in the courtroom after giving evidence until the verdict. I wouldn't want to be there, she said, although I was welcome to sit in any time.

I should have asked her questions, and I thought of a million when I got home, but I was incapable of processing everything she said and at the same time thinking a step ahead. I was exceptionally quiet and they were worried I wouldn't be able to do it however much I reassured them I would turn up and do my best. With the information overload I'd gone to the vacant place in my head and didn't know how to get out of it quickly. I knew I would be a zombie for a few days while my insides processed the details. Only then would I think of questions to ask. I couldn't believe our next meeting would be in the courtroom with the trial underway and her wearing a silly wig and asking me questions on the stand. Thinking that brought on the shaking and I phoned Mum to make me an appointment with the GP. I was going to need something to stop me having a panic attack or passing out on the stand.

I couldn't wait for my next appointment with Judy to get some perspective on how to follow this through because I was seriously doubting I had it in me. For the first time I thought maybe I couldn't do it, that maybe I shouldn't have agreed to do it. I was totally terrified about every aspect of it and I wanted to crawl under a rock and stay there.

Chapter Ten

I sensed the reality of court was sinking in for Phil, and although he professed with confidence he wasn't nervous about giving evidence I could tell he was lying; I knew him. Our relationship had slowly disintegrated into a series of dodgy phone calls and disastrous weekend visits at my parents' house. After The Terrible Tuesday he stayed with me in Ireland for two weeks and then went back to London, to work, moved into a new flat and tried to get on with his life. I cried every night when he went home because I knew deep down things would never be the same between us again – how could they be? I didn't know for sure we wouldn't make it, but in my heart I was never going back to London to live and work, and I couldn't imagine how things would continue without me living in the city we once both loved.

Phil was in a band, loved playing live gigs and was an excellent guitar player. We talked about him moving to Ireland but that meant him giving up his music, and I wouldn't have expected or wanted him to do that, not for me. He was a city boy at heart, not someone who would settle happily into the quiet life of a small town. No matter the different scenarios in my head, our relationship working just didn't add up. We had never talked marriage or children, and I honestly didn't know if we ever would have but we loved each other before The Terrible Tuesday, of that I had no doubt, but there was no denying the cracks in our relationship were getting bigger by the day and it was obvious that neither of us was sure we had a viable future together. Phil was moving on and leaving me behind, and it broke my heart.

I think differently now. I tell myself he didn't have much of a choice, that his options were to sink with me or swim ashore. He tried his very best to swim and I don't blame him for it. It was a truly abhorrent thing that came between us and we were both desperately trying to deal with it on our own. Although we couldn't find any common ground or happy medium to support each other, we did try. We talked about our future often but both were reluctant to commit to anything solid. We fought constantly and couldn't find the easiness we had once shared. We decided to try for some semblance of togetherness at the trial but after that we would take a break to work out how we each felt.

Each of us needed space – as if six months living in different countries wasn't enough. We couldn't agree on the state of our relationship or decide what was right for us until the trial was over. I couldn't even think about it, my emotions were all over the place, and it required too much energy that I just didn't have. I didn't think about how it was affecting Phil. He appeared to be coping well, busy with the normal everyday stuff I once took for granted. I bitterly resented him for having the luxury of everyday life.

Christmas, my favourite time of year, was round the corner. That year, however, I was consumed with worry about the trial. We had already booked our flights and accommodation: Anne, my parents and some of my brothers were coming for the day. Most of the chicks were coming too and I was so pleased. The decision was theirs but I was so grateful they were coming to support me, although I was anxious about them all seeing Him at the same time.

My lovely wee English friends, Rachel and David, Stephanie, Eric and my friend from Leicester, were coming too. I shopped for suits and appropriate clothing for giving evidence and even had my hair done. I still had no desire whatsoever to know what I looked like, so I brought a friend along to be a mirror.

I didn't remember much about Christmas or my twenty-ninth birthday – they passed in a haze of worry and stress, but I distinctly remember eating three boxes of Quality Street. I bought them and kept them in my bedroom, even eating the ones I wasn't particularly fond of – the coffees and toffees. I didn't care. There was just something about Quality Street – the smell when you open the box for the first time and the memories of having them in the house every Christmas as a child. By the time January came round, however, I could hardly fit into my trial clothes; enough was enough.

I avoided new year celebrations and watched television with my parents instead. A far cry from a London New Year's Eve but I was comfortable, safe and very fucking glad to see the back of 2006. I missed work, friends and my London life. Christmas was also my favourite time of year to be at work. People don't usually like working the holidays but I genuinely didn't mind. We dressed up as Santa Claus for the children and the excitement on the ward on Christmas morning was overwhelming. We made the best of the day for the kids and their families with plenty of delicious food and party music. How could you not delight in the joy it brought others?

I wondered how all my kids at work were, but I didn't have the energy for bad news and tried not to ask or think of them. I felt I had abandoned them and their parents but I just couldn't comfort anyone else. It was another thing He had taken away from me and it made me furious. I had worked so hard for so long but now it almost seemed like a waste of time.

Although we were all ready to go, in the literal sense of the word, I didn't feel ready, not emotionally anyway. I still couldn't get my head round what I had to do or how the fuck I was going to do it. Then out of nowhere John rang and said there was a delay with the trial, that it was now scheduled for 12 February. 'What's the delay?' I asked him in despair. He couldn't tell me – it might compromise the case. The nerve! All he said was that it was our side who had asked for an extension, and that it had been granted was very important. I was at my friend's house when John rang, and I dreaded going home to tell my family the news.

They asked a million and one questions I didn't have the answers to. It was all extremely frustrating but what could I or anyone else do? The flight money was wasted as the tickets couldn't be exchanged, so my father had to dig deep yet again and rebook them. As a family we sat down and discussed our lack of information on the trial. We debated questions that we emailed to John: was there any physical evidence of the rape or was it just my word against His? Was there likely to be any more delays because we couldn't afford to throw money down the drain? Did He have any previous burglary or rape convictions? Was His family going to be in court and would they be sitting with mine? What chance did we have of winning? These were basic questions we felt we were owed the answers to. My daddy turned to me and said he wanted me to know that I didn't have to do it and that no one would think any less of me if I couldn't do it. They would fully support me even if I changed my mind. My mummy sat there and never said a word; I knew she wasn't of the same opinion.

'Do you seriously think I should let Him away with it, Daddy?' I asked him.

'You have to realise that it can't solely be down to you, Alana. It isn't your responsibility alone – the police have a case against Him. I'm only asking, are you sure?'

'I'm not sure of anything right now, but I feel I have to try,' I said and meant it.

He looked me in the eyes. 'What if it doesn't go your way? What's going to happen if He walks out of the courtroom at the same time you do?'

I couldn't allow myself to think that. 'I have to believe that won't happen or all this is pointless.' I had to think positive or I couldn't go on with the endless struggle in my head. I couldn't imagine life if we got a not-guilty verdict, and it was best not to imagine it at all because I couldn't cope with it.

'Good,' Daddy said. 'I was just checking.' Mummy nodded in approval.

'What?' I said to her.

She raised her hands defensively, 'Nothing! I knew you'd say that but we had to ask. You know yourself, you have to do it … I for one am looking forward to it.'

I hadn't given much thought to how my mummy was going to cope with the trial. She usually coped with everything in her path without too much fuss, but she was exceptionally angry at Him and I was concerned at how it would pan out in court. I added it to my list of other concerns, of which there were quite a few.

I was worried their opinion of me might alter after they'd actually seen Him. What would everyone think of me? I was paranoid I had made Him out to be this giant monster when in reality He looked like any other normal bloke. If He had lost weight in prison, He wouldn't be as big as He looked in my head and at my bedroom door. I worried my family would think less of me for not fighting a bit more. Many times I thought I should have fought a bit more for what I gave Him.

How I could have fought back, I had no idea, but the guilt stayed with me. I told myself it couldn't be undone or changed no matter how much I wished it could. Judy told me about survival instincts. That my mind was firmly in survival mode, but it didn't make me feel any better about it. I still *let* Him do it. The reason: because I didn't want Him to kill me, but that didn't bring much comfort. Those destructive thoughts coalesced in my mind until one night before the trial I finally snapped. I couldn't hold it together any more. I was so utterly consumed with guilt over what I'd let Him do that I confided in a dear friend, talking for hours about it on the phone until I couldn't speak any more. When my parents finally went to bed I got up for a smoke.

As if he sensed my pain, my father was by my side. I could do nothing but weep at the kitchen table trying to explain how I felt. 'You have to accept what has happened,' he said. 'Accept that you cannot change it and let it go before it eats you from the inside out.' We sat at the table until the sun came up. Me mostly crying and chain-smoking while Daddy made tea and told me the same thing repeatedly: 'You had no choice in the matter, none whatsoever.'

When I heard 'rape' on television swiftly accompanied by 'murder', I often wonder would that have been my fate? Was He capable of murder – of *my* murder? I certainly believed it at the time. I was convinced He was going to kill me, because He said He would, if I didn't do what He demanded. Did those less fortunate girls on the news fight to the death or were they going to die either way? I drove myself to distraction thinking about it at night alone in my bed. The dark hours were not a time to be rational about such things, and in the end I had to go with just still being alive. I was glad to be alive with a second chance at life. A lot of people didn't get that. I had to make peace with my actions, or lack of them, on that inauspicious morning. I just hoped my new-found sense of peace would hold up to scrutiny at the trial.

I saw my GP and explained my looming journey to London. I asked for something to help with the awful panic attacks, the nausea, the vomiting, the shaking, the diarrhoea, the vacant staring episodes and my heart beating so loudly in my ears that I couldn't hear anything else. 'I can't be on the stand like a deaf dead person, now can I?' I tried to kid.

He looked at me like I'd truly lost it. I told him I knew he wasn't a magician but those were my symptoms when I thought or talked about it, and was there anything that could help me. 'Oh … oh, ahem. Right,' he muttered. I'd shocked him. He handed me a prescription and sent me on my way with best wishes, encouraging me to let him know the verdict. 'I truly hope it goes your way, Alana.'

I had to get out of there. 'Right, Doc, will do, and ta very much for the pills!' I said with as much enthusiasm as I could muster while making my exit.

John's answers to our long-debated questions arrived. First was his sincerest apologies that he couldn't discuss the case with us. *Fantastic.* We had to be patient and wait another month to find out at the same time as everybody else. There was no point in being frustrated about it – a waste of my precious time and energy, and being angry about the workings of the justice system wasn't going to change anything either. I understood that everyone deserved a fair trial and all that malarkey – I got that just fine, but it didn't give any thought to the victims and what they went through. I didn't like using 'victim' when talking about myself but I couldn't deny that's what I was. I understood all too well why a large percentage of women didn't give evidence in court. It was the most daunting task I'd ever faced, and I wished I could live with not doing it, but in my heart it was the only way forward, and, Jesus Christ, I really wanted to move forward.

Judy and I discussed the delay at my next appointment. She thought it was a good thing for me in particular: it gave me more time to prepare. Yes, I could do with more time to get ready but I didn't think any amount of time would be enough. I was prepared but unsure if I would ever be ready. I told her John agreed that she could accompany me to court, and I was ecstatic when she cleared her schedule to be at the trial for the entire week. If nothing else, I wouldn't have to remember every little detail to relay when I got home. Helpful as my memory was a bit fucked. I had trouble retaining information from one week to the next and consistently forgot things – most annoying, especially during bloody driving lessons.

Chapter Eleven

Driving lessons were a must as I couldn't delude myself that Dad fancied chauffeuring me around forever. Our next-door neighbour was an instructor and as I was comfortable getting in the car with him, he took me for lessons. Despite being at ease, learning to drive was extremely stressful with my fuzzy brain. In hindsight, perhaps it wasn't the right time to put any extra pressure on myself. I was incapable of remembering things from one lesson to the next and I saw the frustration on my instructor's face when I asked, 'Sorry, which one is the clutch?' for the zillionth time. My parents watched in despair as I stalled at least five times trying to get out of our driveway.

I took two lessons a week to see if that brought an improvement, but no luck. I couldn't imagine mastering the art of simultaneously doing so many things: clutch, accelerator, handbrake, looking in the mirror, remembering to signal and, of course, not forgetting to steer the bloody wheel. The biting point eluded me every week and I was convinced it went to the vacant place in my head just to laugh at me. Some days I couldn't face the lesson and cancelled, but all that achieved was making the next one much worse. The only time I broke out in a sweat now was during my disastrous driving lessons, but on the bright side at least Mum and I had a good giggle about how awful I was when I got home.

My trial was only two weeks away when John told me he didn't think Judy should attend court, that the defence could use it against me and make her testify about my state of mind. In his view, it would be for the best if she wasn't there at all. I couldn't help but be completely enraged. I cried with anger, frustration and disappointment, and was confident that if he requested the fucking Queen to be present he would somehow get her there. I didn't understand his reasonings to justify his decision: how could Judy testify to my state of mind on The Terrible Tuesday when I hadn't even met her yet? I had no fucking need for a psychotherapist before that bloody day and my state of mind since then wasn't what was on trial. *He* was on trial, not me! Had everyone forgotten that small point? John said there was no point risking it at that late stage – surely I could understand? If he'd been in front of me, I would have punched his lights out. I was astounded at how violently angry his news had made me – I'd never been violent towards anyone, not even close to thinking about it! As I listened to John I decided I'd had enough of the whole charade and it hadn't even begun yet. I felt the bitter sting of disappointment again when I found out my beloved brother Paul couldn't make the trial either; he had work commitments in Sweden.

Judy later told me I didn't really connect with my anger despite it being such a powerful emotion. She asked if I was afraid of it. I couldn't help but feel sorry for myself as well as anger at the entire world and everyone in it for being put in this situation in the first place. 'Oh, yes! I'm very afraid of anger,' I told Judy defiantly. 'I'm also very afraid of not expressing it in the right way or towards the right person. I'm not in control of my emotions and anger isn't a good emotion not to be in control of.' Some days I just had to go to the vacant place in my head and switch off completely because I didn't know what to do with my anger. Judy and I made an arrangement that we would speak three times during the week: once after I gave my evidence, once after He gave His and once after the verdict. That would have to do. We continued with my shamanic work and continued asking for guidance in dealing with my emotions and in expressing them. I was growing more comfortable with journeying to the other worlds and it had a calming effect on me, although I was still slow at putting it all together or even fully realising the deeper significance of what I was doing.

The week before the trial began I journeyed asking for strength, guidance and anything else that would support me through the legal process. Judy suggested journeying to the upper world but I wasn't confident enough in my abilities after revolving within the lower world and growing familiar with that path. However, I tried. I met Cat at the entrance to the tunnel and we took a different turn. The wind suddenly lifted us up to the next level, and the ground that appeared before us was cloudy and misty but cleared to show trees, birds and a beautiful lake surrounded by grass. It was difficult to describe because it took place in my head, but it felt so real. We met Keith sitting on a rock in the sun, and we sat beside him enjoying the sunshine together. He turned and told me to trust and believe in myself. If I did that, everything would be okay. He pointed to a path and suggested walking down it. We took the path down through some trees until a house appeared in our midst. It had a large garden with many more animals including galloping wild horses and a large snake. The snake slid up to me making the figure eight around me. To my great surprise, I felt no fear.

I took the key from the plant pot at the front door of the house, not at all phased that I somehow knew where it was, and let myself inside. I carefully walked around the house noting the furniture in every room but empty picture frames. I searched the house from top to bottom but didn't meet anyone, so I walked through the kitchen and down the steps to the basement, finding myself in an interesting room full of bits and bobs — more like a shop than a room in an otherwise normal house. The fire in the hearth was lit, so I took a seat beside it and stayed there for a while.

A purple curtain divided the room, and I was almost afraid of what I would find behind it. Ignoring my apprehension, I pulled back the curtain to reveal a lady. She looked Egyptian and had her hair covered in a scarf and tattoos across her arms. I asked her who she was. She looked at me intensely. 'You are me.' When she uttered those words it was as if she told me she was a part of my soul, the very inside of me. She held my left hand in hers and pins and needles came down the left side of my body. We smiled at each other. She held my hand again and the same odd sensation of pins and needles went down the left side of my body onto the cushions on the floor.

I heard the callback signal of the drums and Cat appeared at the doorway telling me it was time for that journey to end. I turned to say goodbye to the woman but she had disappeared while still holding my hand. I felt she was still holding my hand and I felt her presence as I retraced my steps back to the tunnel. I said my farewells to Cat and she wished me all the best for the coming weeks before I returned up the tunnel and out through the hole in the tree. I took my eyepatch and headphones off and sat up holding out my left hand for Judy to feel. I still had pins and needles in it and it was warm to touch. I held out my right hand for her to feel in comparison. It was cold. 'Oh, Judy,' I said, 'I think I found her.' This was spiritually significant for me because in shamanic terms it was soul retrieval – I'd just found the part of me that had been missing since The Terrible Tuesday; the part that went walkabout when I was in my bedroom thinking I was going to die, the part that disappeared the exact moment the light went out behind my eyes. I was terribly proud of myself having done it at all.

It all sounded a bit weird, and maybe even a bit crazy, but it wasn't about how it sounded or what it was. It was about how I felt, and it made me feel good. In fact, it made me feel great. I felt more like myself than I had done for almost eight months. I felt strong and focused, like I'd just achieved something big. I wanted to jump up and down and laugh and cry all at the same time. I was overcome with joy, and not only that but also with relief that maybe I wouldn't always be demented by the terribleness of it, that I wouldn't always be vacant in the head and shaky with fear. Maybe I could move round it. At the very least I could *try* and move round it. There was such a shift within me that anything was possible. The significance of the journey wasn't lost on me this time. It was exactly what I needed at exactly the right time. I cried uncontrollably as I hugged and kissed Judy, I couldn't thank her enough, and she wished me well for the trial. My tears continued on the walk home, only they weren't tears of sadness. That strength stayed with me over the next few days, and I was not only prepared for the trial but also, for the first time, I was ready: ready in my head and ready in my body. I knew it was going to be tough and that we might not get a guilty verdict, but I was confident I could do everything in my power to make sure we did. And that was all I could do.

I finally looked in the mirror and was delighted to see that my eyes were more like mine, with more fire and more light. I was also a bit more with it and a bit more organised in my head. I'd changed over the last eight months and I wondered if He would recognise me in the courtroom. I hoped not. I couldn't see what He could see, so I may never know the answer to that question. I had lost weight, my hair was longer and a different colour, which would happen quite often depending on my mood – I'm usually blonde but had dyed it a boring brown in an effort to blend into the background. Now, looking in the mirror, I decided it was time to cut and lighten it. I didn't look too bad and I wasn't going to hide away for His benefit. There would be more people than Him in court – a lot of whom had done a significant amount of hard work on my behalf, and I was going to show them I was okay, that I was in fact coping. I wanted to look good on the outside in the hope it would divert attention from what was going on inside my head. I felt more together than I had for a long time. 'I'm ready,' I told my reflection as the *Rocky* theme tune played on repeat in my head.

——————⁓⁓⚬⚬⚬⚬⚬⚬⚬⚬⚬⚬⚬⚬——————

I was still nervous but thankfully didn't have a panic attack at the airport and felt safe in the knowledge I had my magic pills from the GP in case I needed them. I brought with me all the good wishes from everyone at home – surely that must count for something too. That Saturday, as I got on the plane, I was already looking forward to my return journey with everything behind me. I was due to check into my hotel and see friends that night. John was coming over to Rachel's to go through some last-minute preparations and for me to read over my statement again – in case I'd forgotten the details of the worst day I'd ever had. Unfortunately they were ingrained in me and were now part of me. However, the devil was in the detail and so I decided to read it for what I hoped would be the last time.

There was a shift in me. I was ready, and for the first time I thought of Him, not with fear, with curiosity. Was He nervous about the trial? Was He nervous about possibly being found guilty? He didn't strike me as the nervous type but it must have crossed His mind He could be staying in prison for a long time. I was confident that even for a man such as He, this was not a pleasant thought. He was so cocky, so sure of Himself, but would He be the same way in the courtroom as He was in my bedroom? I thought not. I hoped to find Him a lot less cocky, a lot less sure of Himself, a lot less in control of the situation and then we would see just how He liked it.

The things that entered my mind on that plane journey were strange. I was reminded of a photograph that appeared in one of the local papers when I was a teenager playing netball at school. Our team had won the Northern

Ireland final and the caption underneath the picture read 'The Underdog Has Their Day!' or something similar. I didn't understand it then, why we were the underdogs just because we'd never won the title before, but I guess the odds weren't in our favour. Now I found myself in a comparable situation. I knew I was the underdog and had a slim chance of winning this battle, but that same determination helped me fight with everything I had.

I had a good team of people who had helped me prepare, and every moment of the last eight months had brought me closer to facing Him again. Had He thought about me at all? He had no idea who I was or of the work I'd done in preparation for our next, what I hoped would be our last, encounter. He was unaware that I was now physically stronger than before because of all my swimming and walking. He was unaware of my intense psychotherapy and how much mentally and emotionally stronger I felt because of it. He was unaware of my shamanic work, of the spiritual development that had taken place in bringing all the scattered pieces of myself together again just so I could stand tall and strong and proud as I spoke my truth to a room full of strangers.

He was also unaware of just how fragile I was and my hope to never expose that side of myself in the courtroom. I wanted to focus on my depth of inner strength and leave my weaknesses behind. I was aware that this whole process might shatter my fragile stability once again but I had to risk it if I was ever to come out victorious. As I took my seat on the plane I laughed when I thought of my father sitting at our kitchen table telling me that His biggest mistake was not breaking into my flat, it was underestimating the girl who was inside it.

My father once told me I was like a dog with a bone: when I wanted something, I would stop at nothing until I got it. I'd been like that for as long as Daddy could remember, but He didn't know that and I was confident He hadn't thought about me like that. I hoped He was stupid enough to think I had no balls. Maybe He thought I was a pushover in my bedroom, and maybe He thought I'd be the same in the courtroom. He had no element of surprise this time, and He didn't realise how lucky He was to have had it the first time He met me. He was banking on me not turning up, as so often happened in rape cases. In hindsight, everyone was slightly panicking that I wouldn't get on the plane and the case against Him would fall apart.

Oh, but I am on the plane.

As we took off I looked out the window and waved goodbye to Belfast, and I found comfort thinking that would be the last time I did that. The very last time I flew from Belfast to London with the trial looming over me. After this it would be over. I sat back. Are you ready, you spineless, cowardly piece of shit? I hope you're as ready as I am because the wind has changed and I'm coming for you, motherfucker.

PART TWO

The Trial

What lies behind us and what lies before us,
Are tiny matters compared to what lies within us.

Ralph Waldo Emerson

Chapter Twelve

I arrived at Rachel's house and we promptly opened a bottle of wine. John called over with my statement and gave us a rundown of the statistics. The facts: ninety-five per cent of rape cases with no physical evidence got a not guilty verdict and we had no physical evidence. Somehow the police had found the used condom outside, hidden in the bushes. For it to be admissible in court, however, nine DNA marker-type things had to match and we only had seven, so it was useless in the courtroom. Also, in a lot of cases women simply didn't turn up at court, and if they did, they were unable to give evidence because of the upset the whole ordeal caused, which didn't surprise me in the slightest. It was difficult to hear that even if we did get a guilty verdict, sentencing would probably be delayed for the defence to submit papers and reports in His favour for lenient sentencing. John told us if He was found guilty, He may only get five to seven years, but, as He had already been in prison for eight months, that counted as time already served.

I was so confused. *Time already served*. I repeated those words over and over in my head but it seemed surreal. What about me? Did I get anything for time already served in this nightmare? He wasn't the only one who had been in a prison cell for the last eight months. I was in a prison of His making and who knew how long I'd have to stay there. On and on more fabulous information was thrown at us: the news that He could be eligible for parole after serving half his sentence, and that in prison one day, a twenty-four-hour period, counted as two days of a sentence. Fucking unbelievable. Did everybody else know this rule? Was it only me who was completely ignorant of such matters? Why was no one else as horrified as me – or if they were, why had something not been done to change it? It was absurd and completely unjustifiable.

'It's just the way it is, I'm afraid,' John told me nonchalantly. That wasn't good enough, least of all for me. Inadequate sentencing accomplished nothing but discouraging people from coming forward and giving evidence against their rapists. I was convinced of it. It made perfect sense that people would be more willing to take the stand if they knew their attacker would get significant jail time – the time they actually deserved for their crime. There was no going back for me with my own ordeal. I certainly wouldn't be over what happened in a couple of years. I couldn't just pick up the pieces of my life and carry on as if The Terrible Tuesday never happened. Perhaps that was unfathomable – the effect The Terrible Tuesday had had on my head, my insides and my life.

I didn't understand why life in prison could equal only twenty-five years, or how eligibility for parole could come after only serving fifteen of them. If you took a life, surely you should stay in prison for all of your natural life? It wasn't as if the murdered person could come back to life after twenty-five years, so why should their murderer be given a second chance? There were exceptions to every rule, but should the general consensus not be that *life* means just that, and the perpetrator spends the rest of their life locked up?

I couldn't help but be frustrated at the irrationality of sentencing in rape cases. It was common knowledge that it took a special kind of person to commit rape, and in my opinion the chances of Him having a change of heart while serving time were slim to none. So why chance letting Him out early just to hurt someone else? Him being sentenced to five years in prison for not only breaking into my home but also raping me in my own bed was a complete disgrace. Yes, He left me alive and breathing, but there was more than one way to skin a cat. I may have my life but He ended it as I knew it and He most certainly killed me on the inside. The darkness that oozed out of Him in my bedroom reached in and turned the lights off inside me, and He didn't only do it the once – he killed me on the inside over and over again; every time I opened and closed my eyes in the beginning it felt like I was still lying on my bed about to breathe my last.

Even seven months later, there was any number of things, day or night, that took me straight back to that moment when I thought it was game over. Something as simple as a sound, a word, anything at all, and that fear triggered inside me – never mind the flashbacks, panic attacks and the memories that tried their hardest to drive me insane. Maybe they should think about all that before sentencing Him for the crimes He committed. Serving fifteen to twenty years for a crime might put you off committing it, but some might consider the risk worth it if they were only sentenced to five years, seven at the most, knowing they could be out in half that time anyway! Is that all I was worth – five years, seven years, *less*? IF we got a guilty verdict and He was sentenced to five years in prison, He could be out in two. That was it, two bloody years. It took me longer to get a degree in nursing, and I'd never broken into anyone's house or intentionally hurt another living soul. It was just so wrong, and not for the first time I thought, what was the point of putting myself through the whole spectacle?

John told us the judge could specify a minimum amount of time to be served should they see fit, but impressed upon us our chances weren't good. It was important we understood that. Believe me – I got it, but I was baffled by the injustice of the system. Twenty-four hours is one day for the rest of the world, so why should it be any different for Him? Amongst all this frustration was that I was only informed of this a mere twenty-four hours before the trial began. Knowing in advance might have made me think differently about giving evidence. I couldn't allow myself to think about that, especially not the verdict. I just wanted to get through Monday and Tuesday, then I could worry about the verdict at the end of the week – if I made it till then. Nerves were well and truly kicking in, so I had a smoke, drank some wine and tried to relax myself into Sunday. I'd given up on the sleeping malarkey for this week; there was just no point in even trying.

———— ∾⌒⊙⌒⊙⌒⊙⌒∽ ————

On Sunday morning Phil and I took ourselves to the hotel. Unfortunately for us, to put it nicely, it was a complete shithole. I'd booked it online and could blame nobody but myself. It didn't take us long to check out and contact John who put us up in a much more respectable place across the road. My poor friends from home decided to stay in the original hotel – it was cheap for the week and they'd already spent a fortune travelling. It didn't take long for Phil and me to have an argument. Tensions were high and we were both nervous about the morning. Neither of us slept much and we got up at six on Monday to prepare for the day.

I made my way downstairs to meet Anne and my parents for breakfast. Anne was shaking and her face was the colour of a corpse. I encouraged her to eat something but to no avail, she was too nervous, so I gave her two of my magic pills from the GP to see if they calmed her down. We continued attempting to eat in silence until it was time to meet the girls and head to the tube station. My English friends were coming from north London and were to meet us at the courthouse. When we arrived at the courthouse John and Julie met us, looking relieved that we'd even arrived. I was immediately led into the witness room with two of my closest friends where Kate, from Victim Support, was waiting for me. The sudden urge to vomit hit me and I asked for the bathroom. Once the jury had been sworn in, the defendant had arrived, my family and friends had been seated, we had lift off.

My pockets were weighed down with healing crystals from a friend and I had a bottle of water in front of me which I used to distract myself taking continuous sips when all I really wanted to do was smoke – the one thing I obviously wasn't allowed to do. The two barristers gave their opening statements and then Phil was called to give his evidence. We weren't allowed to talk to each other now until I had given my evidence too. John came in and asked me to draw an outline of my flat for the jury. My friend told me I'd forgotten something and I nearly bit her head off in anger until, that is, she told me what I'd missed: the bathroom door. I'd forgotten to draw the bathroom door. In hindsight, it was probably because I had some difficulty getting out of it. I quickly pencilled it in and we sat in silence.

They broke for an hour's lunch signalling the close of the never-ending morning. I wouldn't be called until the afternoon now. John organised food for us in a nearby restaurant, and once settled my daddy graciously filled me in on the morning's events. He immediately said that the barrister had gone through every detail of The Terrible Tuesday, every detail, so I wasn't to worry about him hearing it when I gave my evidence. It sank in that it wasn't just him, it wasn't just my daddy, that actually everyone in the room had heard it. I was instantly embarrassed and relieved at the same time. Telling me this was part of the barrister's strategy would have been helpful – it would have saved me six months of worrying about my father having a cardiac arrest in the courtroom. Daddy continued, telling me he didn't give a shit what happened this week because after seeing Him it was apparent how easily I could have been killed. I was lucky to be alive and my dad didn't care if He walked out of the courtroom at the same time as us as long as we got home safely.

My friends were equally horrified at the size of Him and asked why I never told them just how big and repulsive He was. I felt the tears come to my eyes – so desperately relieved at their reaction. It made me feel so much better about what had happened. They repeatedly told me just how lucky I was, but I didn't feel lucky that day. All I could concentrate on was how genuinely terrified I was at the prospect of seeing Him again and whether I was going to get through it at all.

Chapter Thirteen

The moment I was finally called to give evidence came. I was led into the courtroom by a small blonde-haired woman whose name and job title escapes me. As soon as she opened the door I felt Him, the dark, nasty presence of Him. My feet suddenly wouldn't do the walking any more and she had to guide me through the door. I was one hundred per cent sure he was the right man now without even having to look at Him. My legs went to jelly and my breath caught in my throat. My stomach jumped up and down and I didn't think I would make it past Him to take my seat. I met my sister's eye and she gave me an encouraging smile. She could tell my legs weren't working properly without having to be told.

I was somehow embarrassed, nervous, panicky and everything all at once. I was aware of the complete silence in the room as everyone took a good look at me. I sat down and swore on the holy Bible to tell the truth, and as I did I tried my best to make eye contact with each member of the jury. I wanted them to see me and know I was telling the truth. I wondered if He would swear on the holy Bible too. He probably would, the lying bastard, but I bloody hoped God wasn't having another sabbatical like the last time I needed him.

The barrister began by asking me rudimentary questions: my name, occupation and other basic information. A red lever arch file was placed on the table in front of me and I was asked to open it. As I did so, I knew the show was over before it had even begun. In front of me were photographs of my flat, and after I scanned each of them I put my hands over my face and started to cry – the one thing I didn't want to do and I managed to do it before we'd even got anywhere near the hard part. The judge asked why I was crying. I apologised for being emotional and said I didn't know there would be photos of the flat and, in particular, the bedroom. I explained my shock at seeing them after all these months and said I was angry I hadn't been forewarned. The judge proceeded to ask all sorts of questions about the flat: why I hadn't seen the mess, the date I was last there, the last time I'd been to work. He found it hard to believe I hadn't set foot inside the flat or been back to work since The Terrible Tuesday. I explained clearly that I didn't want anything from inside the flat, anything He had touched, and so Phil's family had cleared it out on our behalf.

This was exactly what the police and barrister wanted: me to break down on the stand and show some emotion – not to be a walking, talking dead person. They could have given me a heads-up about the photographs though. Even if prepared I would have cried at the sight of them. I could see how badly the flat was trashed, much worse than I remembered. It certainly looked like a crime had taken place, and the bedroom was in an inconceivable state. I was talked through every room in the flat and, again, the judge seemed surprised I didn't know exactly what items were missing from what room. I told him I couldn't be sure because I couldn't see at the time of the attack, and afterwards I didn't want anything from the flat except the jewellery I wore to my sister's wedding, my iPod and my mobile phone, none of which could be found.

The barrister took me through that morning: the noise, the bedroom door opening, the dressing gown, the countless times we went round the flat looking for money and other valuables, the pin numbers, the violence, me telling Him I wanted to go home and that I didn't want to die. We talked through how He sat on me – practically suffocating me, the swearing, the threats and the command not to fix myself on the bed; every single detail in my statement was discussed. She took me right up to Him saying, 'I may as well have a quick go while I'm here.'

The barrister was a pleasant woman with a warm tone to her voice but she gave no indication we had previously met. The layout of the courtroom instantly frustrated me because I couldn't look at her while she asked me questions as He was sitting directly behind her and I didn't want to look at Him. I truly didn't want to see His face again. I wasn't ready. I put my hand up to the side of my face to block Him from my side view and faced the jury, directing my answers at them instead. I wanted to apologise to them all for the horrors they were about to hear but I couldn't speak freely to do so.

The judge asked me a couple of times if I wanted a break but I was emphatic in my denial. I wanted to push on and get the ordeal over with. I didn't acknowledge His presence in any way other than to keep my face averted from Him at all times. The judge called it a day at five and warned me not to talk to any other witnesses overnight. He asked if I could wait in my seat so he could instruct security to take Him to the holding cell before I got up from the stand. I smiled gratefully appreciating his thoughtfulness. This saved me from walking past Him again and, to be honest, I couldn't have stood up even if I had of wanted to – my whole body had gone to jelly. I was shaking, sweating and incredibly thirsty, but the first day was over and that had to count as progress.

Once He was removed everyone waited for me to get up. I couldn't feel my legs and the room spun when I stood up. I had to lean on the table and take a couple of deep breaths to stop from passing out. I walked through the courtroom transfixed by the sight of His family standing behind the plastic enclosure where He had been sitting. Walking at a snail's pace, my legs as if on stilts, I saw a woman I instantly knew was His wife and another woman shooting me daggers, maybe a sister. There was a man, maybe a brother, and lastly I saw a very young boy wearing a Burberry-check tie who I knew was His son. There were other young faces amongst the crowd and I was horrified by their presence. Children, His children, had been brought to court. Everything was in slow motion as I walked past them.

I asked John if he knew there were children in court. He did. I explained how inappropriate it was for His children to be there and said how extremely uncomfortable I felt. Although John told me nothing could be done about it, surely there was a rule about children in court? I was worried the children would hear about their father and the effect it would have on them – despite me knowing it to be the truth.

I loved working with children. They kept everything so simple. They hadn't yet developed the ability to lie or deceive, and they usually showed their emotions on their faces. His children wouldn't have the emotional maturity to deal with what they heard in court that week, and I was angry and felt somehow responsible for wrecking whatever opinions or feelings they had for their father. His children's presence was just another part of the awfulness which I couldn't undo. John didn't seem to understand how much it disturbed me and I couldn't wait to talk to Judy tomorrow.

———•◦◦◦◦◦◦———

We returned to the hotel and arranged to meet up in the bar. Some ate, some didn't. I had reverted to not tolerating food in my mouth, much less in my stomach, and just had a drink instead. No alcohol however – I was holding it together by a very thin thread and alcohol might have sent me over the edge. Daddy again took us through the day's proceedings. He's a great storyteller and holds an audience captive even through the most unpleasant of stories. Some of the girls hadn't been in the courtroom the whole time, so at least this kept everyone in the loop. My dad said that Phil's dressing gown had been admitted into evidence with bits cut out where they had found semen. They were unable to identify whose semen it was, but it was semen all the same. Phil had faced some difficult questions about our sex life and whether he had seen the condom wrapper that was found on the floor of our bedroom. Phil had been clear it wasn't there when he left for work and that he'd never seen it. The defence barrister obviously suggested it was ours all the same. It wasn't, of course, but the suggestion would stay with the jury.

I felt overwhelming pity for Phil. I knew just how shy he was talking about things of a sexual nature with me, never mind a room full of people and especially my father. I just felt naked. Exposed. Neither Phil nor I would ever choose to discuss our sex life with friends never mind strangers, and it made me so angry that the defence barrister was freely permitted to ask Phil such intrusive questions, questions that had no bearing on the truthfulness of The Terrible Tuesday.

I had a sinking feeling in my stomach that a similar fate was in store for me tomorrow. I knew the barrister would embarrass me by asking personal questions and anger me with her invasiveness. It was none of anybody's business, and I felt the annoyance prematurely building up inside me. I could only hope I could keep a lid on it until I'd given my evidence. I wasn't the only one who was angry – I could hear it in the voices around the table and I could feel it in the air. He had sat in court in a dodgy tracksuit slouched over His chair. Far worse, He had had the audacity to wink and smile at my mother. She wanted to kill Him while He acted like He was bored by what was taking place around Him. He was just as cocky as I'd remembered. Everyone reiterated just how large they thought He was, and it was then I knew the nightmare was just beginning for most of them. Seeing Him was like adding the last piece of the jigsaw and completing the picture. Collectively, our group felt disturbed, upset and incredibly tired but Anne was the worst.

Her face was a horrible green colour that had stayed all day, and she had been physically sick, so disgusted was she by His presence. She had a vacant look and it was obviously very difficult for her to hear the events so explicitly detailed. It took a whole bottle of rosé before she could speak properly and once that was gone she was promptly put to bed. I was so grateful to everyone for being there with me and I hoped that together we could make it through the week without anyone, including me, having a breakdown. We had an early night, my sister staying in my room. She snored from the combination of my prescription pills and the wine but I didn't mind at all. Instead, I was comforted by the familiar, rhythmic noise she made while I still couldn't sleep. Roll on another terrible Tuesday.

—————∿◦◦◟◠◝◦◟◠◦◦∿—————

Tuesday morning shone brightly into my room but I could hardly muster the energy to get out of bed. I asked God and every angel, saint and spirit guide under the sun for help. Eventually I just had to get out of bed and get ready to go. We met downstairs for breakfast only to not eat anything once again. Everyone was more anxious than yesterday and conversation was limited. We knew what was coming and it was always going to be the worst part for me. I assured my father he could leave at any time but he point-blank refused. I gave my sister more pills but decided against taking any myself because I really needed my wits about me. My solicitor friend had read my statement and was worried about the key-in-the-door scenario. She said it was the only inconsistent part of the statement, and she would question me about it, without a doubt, if she were working for the defence. She defended people like Him all the time and I didn't know that side of her at all. She has such a sweet nature and a kind way that I couldn't imagine her inside a courtroom defending the likes of Him.

The key was found on the other side of the door, and she asked me how I could see through the keyhole that the front door was open if the key was in the lock on the other side of the door? I wasn't sure how to answer her except to be truthful about what I saw. It was one of those old locks that had a round knob to open the door and I could still see through it even with the key in it. I saw light shining in and I didn't realise the key was on the other side. When I realised I was locked in, I bent down and looked through the keyhole and saw the front door open. Because we had closed the front door previously, I assumed He had left and taken the key with Him. That was the truth and I had nothing more to add. 'Refute everything she says to you,' my friend instructed me. 'Everything she suggests that's not true say, "That's not the truth. That's not the truth!" Don't let her suggest something and leave it out there as a possibility for the jury.' I was so impressed by how professional she sounded that I didn't know what to say except agree that I would do as she said. I hoped to remember that when I got on the stand.

The shaking started before we'd even left the hotel. We got the tube again and walked the rest with a stop at Starbucks. I practically cried until I was allowed to order my own coffee as I was sure someone would get my order wrong. I'm very fussy over Starbucks, something I'm sure most can relate to. Grande, skinny, sugar-free vanilla latte, extra hot and easy on the foam. The sort of order that makes the barista roll her eyes and think, 'What a dickhead.' What can I say? I like it how I like it and today of all days I needed it to be right.

All too soon we were at the courthouse and it was time once again to get the show on the road. Fucking Tuesdays, I hated them.

Chapter Fourteen

The judge instructed my barrister I was to tell the next part in my own words – she wasn't to help or direct me in any way. He then turned back to me asking what happened next. I couldn't breathe. I quickly explained that I couldn't look at the jury for this part and I apologised but I just couldn't. I told them everything about the rape without looking at them: I told them about the breathing and the shoving and the pushing and the pulling. I told them I said no and begged Him not to do it to me. I told them what position I was in and what parts of me He touched without my permission. I told them how He held His hand at my throat and squeezed so hard I couldn't breathe; how I thought I might have choked on my own vomit and that I had wondered if that happened would He still be liable for my murder. I told them about the dressing gown coming loose – how I saw Him with a stocking over His face which terrified me more. I told them I pulled the dressing gown back down over my head because I couldn't bear to watch Him.

The judge offered me a break but I told Him I'd rather continue – once I was finished, I was going to lose it completely, so I needed to get through it in one sitting. Deep breaths. I told them He took Himself out of me and massaged Himself and then forced Himself inside me a second time. I told them about His breathing and the disgusting noises He made. I told them I thought I was going to die. I told them how I knew He was finished.

I should have told them about my pain on the inside but I didn't. I should have told them there were moments when I truly lost myself inside my own head but I didn't. I should've told them about the darkness oozing out of Him that reached in and turned the lights off inside me but I didn't. I should have told them He enjoyed raping me but I just couldn't bring myself to tell them that.

I told them I heard Him taking the condom off and zipping up His jeans. That He told me to get up and go to the bathroom. I told them my legs wouldn't work and I couldn't see, so He half carried me banging me into the walls on the way. I told them He held me under the shower until I was clean. That He told me He would be back in fifteen minutes to kill me and I had better not make a sound. I told them I waited a few minutes before turning the water off, getting out of the shower and taking the dressing gown off my head only to realise I was locked in the bathroom.

I attempted a sip of water. I was half crying and shaking, and I knew I had to take a break before I was physically sick. My mouth was watering and I wouldn't be able to swallow it back for much longer. My barrister asked me about the key, the door and the lock, as was expected. I gave my explanation, sticking to the truth as I'd planned. She seemed satisfied with my turn of events. I told them about the nursing scissors and getting the screws out. About pulling on the door with everything inside me and then making a run to the nuns' house. She asked me a couple more questions before the judge interrupted to say we needed to break before cross-examining began.

I looked up at the jury for the first time since I began speaking. Some of them wouldn't look at me and I was overcome with embarrassment after what I'd just told them. Every part of me was mortified and I just wanted to go home. Looking at them all, I was excruciatingly, painfully aware that it was rock bottom for me, again. I was totally and utterly broken – which was bad enough happening in front of everyone but worse in front of Him. No verdict could change Him seeing me like that. Whatever strength I had before this morning had left me and I didn't know how to get it back.

He was swiftly removed from the room before I was helped down from the stand – I could hardly stand up never mind walk. I snuck a look at my parents: my father looked okay but a little weary and my mother looked like she would kill Him with her bare hands. She was still watching the spot where He had been sitting. My sister was once again green, shaking and visibly heartbroken for me. I couldn't bear to look at anyone else and made a run for the bathroom.

My friends, those who weren't in the courtroom, ran after me. I had a meltdown right there in the cubicle. Retching, puking, shaking, crying and pulling at my hair. I told myself over and over that I couldn't do any more. I couldn't go back in and see all those people again. I just couldn't do it. I sat on the floor with my head over the toilet bowl just not able to get up. Nothing worked – not my legs or my arms, and now that I'd really started crying I couldn't stop. Kate from Victim Support asked the judge for an extended break while Julie ran off to tell John what was happening.

My friends lifted me from the floor and one took me over to the sink, washed my face and fixed my make-up. As she finished she leaned in and very quietly whispered, 'I know you can do it. You're the strongest person I've ever met. It's almost over. You just have to hang in for another short while. Just once more. Go in there one more time and get this over and finished with. The worst part is over.'

I looked up at her, 'Oh, no,' I said. 'The worst is yet to come.'

She took no heed of my apprehension. 'I know you can do it,' she said. Her quiet words calmed me in all the madness. She wasn't panicking and she wasn't nervous. She had total and utter faith that I would finish what I had started, I saw it in her eyes. It would all have been for nothing if I gave up now, so I gathered all my physical and mental strength and tried hard to control my breathing and stop shaking. 'Let's have a quick cigarette,' I said, 'and then I'll go back in and finish it.'

We went outside to my family and the rest of my friends. My mummy gave me a kiss and told me she loved me with tears running down her face. My daddy hugged me and I started to cry again. I told him I desperately wanted to go home but he assured me I was nearly there and couldn't give up now. Anne made her way towards me and it was all I could do to stop her in her tracks. If she talked to me or held me, I wouldn't be able to keep it together. We didn't stand outside for much longer as I'd have lost the will to keep going if I'd had more time to think. We had to go back inside now or I would never finish it.

We were called back into the courtroom and the judge asked me if I was able to continue. 'Yes, I am,' I responded. It was His barrister's turn to question me and she started off gently enough with the sequence of events, then asked me about my sex life and choice of contraception which I have no choice but to begrudgingly answer. Proceedings quickly took a turn for the worse as she suggested I was running 'scantily clad' about my bedroom. She was on a fucking roll and I was instantly incensed not only that she dared to make such a ridiculous comment but that she threw it out there at the get-go. I was no longer upset or ashamed, just insanely angry with her audacity. I kept control in my voice when I answered, 'No, I wasn't running scantily clad about my bedroom. I was appropriately dressed for being in my bed as I was asleep at the time,' taking my friend's advice and refuting everything she said that wasn't true. I looked the members of the jury in the eyes every time I refuted one of her claims. On and on she continued, and it descended into an almost laughable escapade when she suggested I feared so badly He was going to rape me that I had imagined it took place; that He had violated me in my head and I had convinced myself He had raped me when He actually hadn't. I almost laughed at her and wished I could have looked at her as she made her ridiculous suggestion. 'I can't believe any woman would *imagine* herself being raped and I certainly didn't imagine it,' I told the jury. 'I am telling you He raped me because He did. I would love it if that were not the truth of the matter, but it is. Every word of it is the truth and I cannot change that.'

She questioned me on what happened in the bathroom, suggesting I went there of my own accord, which anyone could see was obviously ludicrous. She pressed me on the key and the lock, what I could have seen and how I must have been mistaken. She was clever in some respects, asking me the same questions in a different manner in the hope of tripping me up. I was getting increasingly frustrated with her and nearly blew the whole thing by losing my temper. I looked at the judge and said I didn't know what she wanted me to say, that I had explained the truth of what I saw: 'I looked through the keyhole and could see that the front door was open.' I clarified that I didn't know the key was on the other side of the door, but as far as I was concerned the fact that it was there changed nothing. If they had seen it for themselves, they'd have known I was telling the truth.

The judge interrupted once more to say he thought I'd answered enough questions on the bathroom door and that there were photographs of both the broken lock and door frame. He also reminded the jury that the key was found on the outside of the door. His barrister had the cheek to once again suggest that the rape had never taken place and I was never locked in the bathroom. I could hardly take any more. I refuted her allegations sternly and assured the jury I was telling the truth. I was shaking again, but not with fear – with anger. I knew I was going to lose my temper with her at any moment.

The judge asked if the barrister had any more questions for me but thankfully she'd finished her interrogation. He was removed from the courtroom and I nearly jumped off my seat to get off the stand. His family threw me dirty looks but this time I looked back at His wife and gave her one of my very own. I gave her absolutely everything I had. You scumbag of a mother making your children listen to this. You should be ashamed of yourself. You, not me, *you* should be ashamed. I nearly took the door off the hinges when I finally made my way out of court.

I went to the bathroom where my friend found me. 'See,' she said, 'I knew you could do it!'

'Oh God, I want to *kill* someone!' was all I could muster in reply.

That was truly awful. It was excruciatingly difficult not to get up and punch that barrister in the face. I sincerely hoped she was never on the end of a violent sex crime and never fully realised how her suggestions made me feel. When her time was up in this world I hoped she looked back and knew she was defending a lying, dirty, evil scumbag and realised it wasn't her finest hour.

We went to lunch with everyone relieved I had finished giving evidence. I was still too angry to eat and was now just looking forward to going back to my hotel room so I could phone Judy. If there was ever a time I really needed to talk to her, it was now. My friends and I made our way back to the hotel and I grabbed the opportunity to contact her. She couldn't get a single word in edgeways as I ranted, raged and cried down the phone with all the shame, anger, frustration and helplessness over the last two days. I was in unstoppable meltdown mode. I was so worried how everyone else was coping that I couldn't vent my anger in front of them, and it was a relief to do it with Judy even if it was only on the telephone. I didn't know how she managed to calm me down before I completely careered over the edge of reason.

The children weren't my responsibility but maybe when this was over I could voice my concerns to John properly, she reasoned. The worst was over now and I'd done what I had committed to doing: telling the truth and speaking from my heart with honesty and courage. The rest of the week was out of my control and I had to accept that and remain confident in the resolution that I'd done my best. I had to accept and acknowledge my limitations so I could concentrate on looking after myself as best as possible for the rest of the week. We were on the phone for over two hours – until I could speak no more. I tried to get some rest before going downstairs to meet everyone to find out about the rest of the day. It was impossible to sleep but lying in the quiet and closing my mind to the horrors of the last few days went some small way to rejuvenating me. I eventually made my way downstairs eager to hear what had been said in my absence, but I was seriously unprepared for the state of everyone when they came back.

'What the hell happened?' I asked them. 'You all look terrible!' My mother was very quietly crying where she stood and my sister was shaking. My dad was the only one able to speak, 'They played the 999 call. I can't lie to you, it was atrocious. Come on, let's get a table and sit down. All of us.' I hadn't realised the recording would be played for everyone to hear but I immediately understood why they were so upset. My mind took me back to supporting myself on Mairead's sink, trying to remain upright while retching and crying and answering questions. It set the sombre mood for the evening.

Mairead had done well giving her evidence and corroborating my version of events. His barrister suggested to Mairead that I was hysterical, probably to further her suggestion of it all being in my head, but Mairead refused to be drawn in and emphatically denied I was hysterical – deeply traumatised but definitely not hysterical. Mairead was excused and after a short break they played the 999 call. I could be heard telling Mairead what had happened and being sick as Mairead repeated the operator's questions to me. They heard me retching, crying and telling Mairead I had already drank water and had a cigarette when the operator informed her not to let me eat or drink anything. The operator could be heard telling Mairead I wasn't to wash, and they heard me say He had held me in the shower washing me before locking me in the bathroom. Anne said I sounded childlike and it was unbelievably distressing and shocking for everyone to listen to, most especially my mother, as I could be heard repeating that I wanted to go home and I just wanted my mummy. The judge had called it a day then and said court would reconvene at nine in the morning which gave everyone food for thought overnight.

Our group was a bit traumatised by Tuesday's events and so all quickly retired to bed. Tomorrow, He would take the stand and God only knew what He had to say for Himself. My anxiety levels were at an all-time high.

On the one hand I was so relieved Tuesday was over but I wasn't looking forward to what tomorrow would bring. Phil stayed with me on Tuesday night. We didn't talk about it too much; we were both simply exhausted. It was extremely stressful for Phil and there was nowhere for him to run and hide. I felt really bad for him, but he told me he was looking forward to Wednesday, to hearing what He would say. Neither of us slept much that night and we headed down early to breakfast where it was abundantly clear no one had slept much at all. I grew more and more concerned about my mother as she was turning the same colour as my sister.

Chapter Fifteen

We arrived shortly before nine and I went into the empty courtroom and sat down. I wanted to sit in on the day's evidence but as I sat alone I realised I wasn't up to staying. I had no desire to hear the lies that would spill out of His mouth and no wish to hear His voice again. As I got up to leave I met my barrister on her way in. I smiled at her and she asked if I was staying. 'No,' I said, 'I'm not. I hope you have a good day.' Outside I told everyone I was going back to the hotel. I was bitterly disappointed in myself but knew I'd made the right decision.

I headed back to the hotel and up to my room and lay down on the bed. I knew I wouldn't sleep but I needed some quiet time. At least this way I could go to the vacant place in my head without anyone worrying about me. It was all getting a bit much – the stress, the anxiety, worrying about everyone and everything I had no control over. I had talked to John about one of the jurors who wouldn't look me in the eye. I was worried she didn't believe me, and it would only take one juror to have doubts in their mind to return a not-guilty verdict. John said he wasn't worried about her, that she had already made up her mind He was guilty. I couldn't understand how he could be so sure and I remained anxious.

If the verdict was not guilty, then it had all been for nothing. I was starting to feel guilty for putting everyone through the week in my quest for justice. *Would this be worth it by the end of the week?* The pressure of it all seeped into my bones and I lay on the bed for hours staring at the ceiling, trying to ignore the nausea and the somersaults in my stomach, trying my best to hang on to whatever nerves I had left in my body and my head. I didn't know what I would do or how I would feel if He got away with rape. I knew He would be found guilty of burglary as He'd admitted to that, so he was going back to prison either way, but it was so important to me that the jury believed me. I wasn't going to be happy with anything less than a unanimous verdict and I wondered if perhaps I was asking too much. I prayed to God for the jurors to see the truth and not be blinded by the lies I was sure He was spinning at that very moment.

Anne phoned at lunchtime to say it had been a busy morning. Andrew had taken the stand as the first police officer on the scene. He had made Anne smile when he told the jury I was in the garden 'pulling profusely' on a cigarette when he arrived, as my family often joked how quickly I smoked a cigarette. The rest of his evidence was routine. He was followed by the doctor from the Havens who took the jury through my time there and at the rape clinic in Whitechapel. The doctor agreed I was extremely upset and deeply traumatised but not hysterical. She told the jury I had repeated my version of events to both her and one of the nurses and she had nothing more to add.

The forensic pathologist then took the stand talking about the bruising I had and how it was consistent with my version of His handling of me. He pointed out thumb and fingerprint marks on my body which correlated with my explanation of how He had pulled and shoved me about the bedroom and the bed. My sister was surprised at how interesting it all was. His barrister then made the mistake of questioning the good doctor's credentials. He immediately shot her down in her seat stating that he was an expert in forensic pathology and bruising, that he had studied my case extremely closely and it was in his *expert* opinion that I was telling the truth. My sister said everyone was really absorbed in the morning's evidence and confident that it supported my version of events. They had broken for lunch before the principal a-hole took the stand in the afternoon. 'Prepare yourself,' I told her. 'It's going to be really bad when He starts talking and you hear His voice.' I asked her how Mummy was doing and she said not that well, but that she was determined to stay and hear His evidence this afternoon. Before we ended the call I made sure to add, 'Leave if you can't take it. I won't mind. Tell everyone I said to just get up and leave if it's too difficult and let me know when you're on your way back.'

This was it. The moment we sank or swam. I sat on the floor of my hotel room and nausea spread over me. I seriously needed some sugar as my energy reserves were so depleted I thought I might faint. I wished I had stayed in court but I knew it would have been a fruitless endeavour. If I was this much of a wreck in my hotel room, what would I have been like when He walked past me to take the stand? I just didn't have it in me to be there. My emotions were all over the place and I couldn't have trusted myself not to lose my temper at His lies or not to shout out in the courtroom that He was a lying fucking bastard and thus ruin the whole case. I had no choice but to put my faith in my lovely barrister and hope God was watching over us and helping.

I remembered the balls the barrister had when we first met and how much she was looking forward to the cross-examination. Well, love, your time has arrived and I wish you well with it. I prayed for hours. I prayed to God, to every angel and saint I could think of, and I prayed to every element of the earth: to the north, south, east and west, to earth, air, fire and water. I asked every god and goddess, every spirit guide and guardian to come together to hear my prayer. Please, God, let my lovely barrister be as vicious and nasty as His was. Please let Him get caught up in His own lies. Please let her trip Him up on the stand and reveal Him to be the lying, evil bastard I know He is on the inside. Please let the jury see Him as I did. Please, I prayed.

———— ∽∾∽⋯⋯⋯ ————

I waited with bated breath and finally Anne rang to say they were on their way back. She wouldn't say anything else, so all I could do was wait. Everyone looked as bad as I was expecting and much worse than the day before. My mummy couldn't be consoled, so my parents went to the chapel at the children's hospital in the hope it might calm her down and help her focus. Everyone was meeting in the hotel bar at seven and there was no point in Daddy going through the day's proceedings twice, so I waited until everyone arrived, got myself a drink and settled down at the huge table to hear the day's events. You could have heard a pin drop when Daddy was talking and it was evident he was as shocked and concerned as everyone else with what the day had brought.

They were firstly shocked by His horrendous attitude – He couldn't even be bothered to sit up properly in the chair while He gave His evidence. His lack of respect and cockiness knew no bounds. He was a burglar by trade He had informed the jury – that's how He made His money, by breaking into people's houses when they were out. He was a crack addict and needed the money to support His addiction. He tried to justify how he earned his money by using his crack habit as an excuse – that it wasn't His fault that was what He did for a living, He had no option. He wasn't deterred by my presence in my own flat. It wasn't His fault I hadn't answered the door nor was it His fault I was in my bed asleep. He needed the money. Yes, He put the dressing gown over my head and, yes, He took me round the flat looking for things to steal and money to take. However, I exaggerated. I exaggerated His language, the violence, the fear – everything about the whole situation. He admitted He may have got a bit carried away when He saw my bank statements and realised I had a credit limit of three thousand pounds because He simply couldn't understand why I hadn't used it. He couldn't understand why I lived within my means and could afford to have money like that on a credit card. He may have been a bit rough, violent and aggressive towards me but He was excited at the prospect of making so much money out of me.

He admitted I suggested He let me get dressed to go to the shop so I could take the money out for Him. He admitted He decided against it as it was just too risky. He basically corroborated my version of events up until the rape. He even admitted I had told Him I wanted to go home to my family in Ireland. He admitted He had laughed at me when I had said that and my barrister asked Him how He felt about that now. He just shrugged His shoulders and said 'And what?' He was too stupid to realise this highlighted His blatant disregard for my feelings eight months ago and now. That was the moment that broke my mother. She understood how desperate I must have felt to tell Him I wanted to go home and was incensed He hadn't given a fuck about it, not then and not now.

He admitted He was looking for a laptop and anything else He could sell on but denied He told me not to cover myself on the bed. The judge then asked Him to clarify what I was wearing for the jury. He admitted He saw condoms in my bedside locker but denied He had touched them. He admitted His phone had rang and that He had tried to tie me up on the bed with the telephone wire but denied He had raped me. It didn't happen, He said, and He was quite emphatic in His denials. He said that because of His crack habit He couldn't get an erection, again, not realising this corroborated my version of events. He admitted He had become a bit nervous because I was breathing 'funny' and He didn't want me to die but denied He had his hand round my throat at the time. He didn't have an answer as to why I couldn't breathe if He didn't have His hand wrapped round my throat.

He admitted He had tried to tie me to the bed but that my funny breathing stopped Him, and He said that I had said I needed the bathroom. He was asked if He had seen the condom wrapper and He said He hadn't. The judge said that the condom wrapper had to be admitted into evidence because, by His own admission, He hadn't seen it when He was there, Phil hadn't seen it and I hadn't seen it but it was there when He left, so that posed the question of where it came from. He didn't have an answer for that even though it was made clear that no one entered the flat from Him leaving until the police arrived. He denied holding me under the shower, denied locking me in the bathroom and denied telling me He was coming back to kill me.

He was rude and arrogant and had to be reminded more than once that He wasn't to interrupt my barrister and was only to speak when He was asked a direct question; that she was the one asking the questions, which pissed Him off considerably, my father said, and I was immensely proud of my barrister and her balls in dealing with Him. He didn't have an answer as to why the key was in the other side of the door or why I had to break out of the door, clearly shown in the photographs, if I hadn't been locked in the bathroom in the first place.

My solicitor friend told me He was a terrible witness but not to get my hopes up. His barrister pointed out that there was no physical evidence whatsoever of rape taking place and that it was quite possible, entirely plausible even, that it didn't happen. That I was so traumatised by the whole experience that in my head it happened but that it physically didn't happen, that I felt violated being manhandled in my own home and by being underdressed. He had admitted He was a criminal in an effort to convince the jury He too had nothing to hide. He had told them everything He had done but had denied rape because, He said, it didn't happen and that was a compelling argument from His side of the fence. His barrister said He knew He was going to prison for burglary, that He'd been in prison before for residential burglary and that He had been honest about that. In doing so she hoped to convince the jury He had denied the rape because it wasn't true, but I sincerely hoped she hadn't managed to convince the jury of any such thing. I hope she was comfortable with who she had made her bed with because if you lie down with a dog, you'll get up with fleas.

My father said at the very least they created doubt in the minds of some of the jury and nobody could call which way it was going to go. It was unfortunate that the condom couldn't be admitted into evidence, and it was also unfortunate that He was so aware of forensics that a complete fingerprint match couldn't be found. Unfortunate or unlucky doesn't cover it, but I was pleased He had let Himself down on the stand. My friend told me that was only because I knew He was a liar and a rapist. That the jury didn't have the luxury of that knowledge and they had to make up their minds based on the evidence that they had heard that week. She didn't want me to be disappointed if it didn't go my way. You did your best, they told me, and we would have to wait and see what happened.

I looked around the table at all those people who had come here for me, who put themselves into the path of true darkness for me; each and every one of them so tired, so shell-shocked and so on edge about the verdict, and I was immensely grateful to them all for being there and in my life. My mother had aged ten years in three days and I'd never seen her so upset. My father was dog-tired and couldn't wait to get home. Anne was in shock, not realising people like Him existed in the world before The Terrible Tuesday. She took it the hardest and had been outside on the phone to my other sister, not bearing to listen to our father go through it all again. She could hardly speak a coherent sentence so confused was she about it all. It had stopped her in her tracks and she would carry the size of Him and the sound of Him and the things He did to me to her grave. I knew this without her having to tell me.

On top of that, it was Valentine's Day and Phil had bought me flowers and a CD and a lovely card. I had nothing to give him. I almost broke down because I knew this was our last Valentine's Day together and I was suddenly overwhelmed with sadness and exhaustion. I had a couple of glasses of wine and fell asleep as soon as my head hit the pillow.

Chapter Sixteen

We made the journey to the courthouse again. This time we were led into a witness room together. John was taking the stand this morning to go through a few formalities, so there was no real need for us to be in court. The judge asked the jury to listen to the 999 call again and then, that was it, it was over, and the jury were sent to their own room for deliberations. Obviously nobody had any idea how long it would take them to reach the final verdict. I felt my heart pounding in my head and I was sure every time the door opened everyone else could hear it too. We went out for lunch and upon returning learned they still hadn't reached a verdict. The jury had Julie phone me to ask how thick the popsocks that were in my drawer were. I had no idea, and all I could tell them was that they certainly weren't thin as I wore them to work, but, again, I couldn't honestly be sure.

I was frustrated I couldn't remember something so minute and also slightly appalled they were asking me questions at this late stage. It meant they really were deliberating. Wasn't it obvious He was a lying bastard? Now I was seriously worried they mightn't come to the right conclusion about Him after all. I didn't think my body could take much more of the waiting. I had nausea, diarrhoea, was sweating profusely and shaking from within. I couldn't think about the verdict at all or I would be physically sick. I was exhausted from trying to keep up the pretence that I was okay when we all knew I really wasn't.

Julie told me we had to prepare a witness impact statement for the court in case He was found guilty. Rachel, Julie and I took ourselves off to a quiet room and went through how each aspect of my life had been affected as a direct result of The Terrible Tuesday. We were as honest as possible and when were finally finished I was devastated at what my life had been reduced to and at what I'd lost in the past eight months. I knew Judy would say what was in black and white wasn't a true reflection of how I was or the progress I'd made in coming to terms with the events of that day, but it didn't bode well for a full recovery or speedy return to a normal life. We went back to the witness room after lunch and continued to wait throughout the afternoon. The tension in the room was palpable and there was very little conversation. I met John in the corridor and he told me to come into a separate room with him. The two girls from Victim Support were there and he told me it was apparent there would be no verdict today but hopefully we should get one tomorrow. I didn't understand what was taking so long.

John asked me if we would come back for sentencing, and I told him we wouldn't be coming back regardless of what happened over the next two days. He told me a bit about the defendant and the investigation. I stopped him and said, 'Please tell this to everybody. They're all about to have a nervous breakdown sitting around waiting for the verdict.' He agreed. My eldest brother had come over for the day and Rachel's lovely daddy had also joined us to show his support. Phil's parents were there and between my family and groups of friends the room was packed to capacity.

We went back to the witness room and I explained that John was going to tell us how he caught Him. They were all enthralled with John and his storytelling. He began by telling us that as soon as he met me in Mairead's garden on The Terrible Tuesday and I told him I had given Him my pin numbers, he realised he could capture the suspect on CCTV making a withdrawal with my bank cards. He called in a favour and pretty soon they had caught Him doing just that. Once they had a couple of clearly identifiable pictures of Him, they soon discovered who He was and where He lived. They had six officers watching His property in thirty degree heat for two days in a van outside his home, sure He would return when He eventually ran out of money. John also added He was extremely well known to the police having had over forty previous arrests for a dazzling array of crimes and had been in and out of prison for many a year. The police were also aware of His crack habit and His penchant for burglary. When He made an appearance on Thursday morning the officers split up, three taking the front of the house and three taking the back. Sure enough,

He split out the back door and it took all six officers to bring Him in. He resisted arrest, which no one seemed surprised to hear.

I was totally engrossed in John's story although appalled He was out of prison in the first place as John told us they had matched His DNA to another burglary in my street not long before. He had cut Himself entering through a small window at the back of the premises and it struck me again how unlucky I was not to have had DNA evidence in my case against Him. He first gave a no-comment interview, and John admitted he was concerned he may only be able to convict Him with handling stolen goods – that was until I remembered His phone ringing in my flat.

At the next interview John used this information to his advantage and asked Him was He aware of satellite navigation? He said of course He was. John then told Him he knew His phone had rung at the time the crime was committed and that satellite navigation placed Him at my flat at the time of the burglary. Not exactly accurate, but He wasn't as knowledgeable about satnav technology as He thought which would, at best, put Him within a twelve-mile radius of my flat at the time of the burglary. It was evident from the very beginning of the story that we had much to be thankful for in having John lead the investigation.

Between the photographs of Him using my bank cards, John asking Him to take part in a line-up and telling Him I had agreed to identify the suspect, it was enough for His solicitor to advise Him to admit He had broken into my flat. This turned out to be a huge mistake on His behalf because John had Him right where he wanted Him – now they were going to charge Him with rape as well as burglary. The case moved quickly forward and the police were as dismayed as we were when the physical evidence proved inadmissible in court – the condom, the condom wrapper and the fingerprint found on the inside of my bedroom drawer as it was only a partial match. The police felt confident in moving ahead though, John told us. I was a nurse, for one, with a clean record and was potentially a strong witness. They felt I could do well on the stand. The first two witnesses in the case were nuns and it was a given that their word would be taken as the truth after swearing on the Bible – John couldn't possibly have written it better himself. The photographs of the bruising cemented my story and so they had contacted the forensic pathologist who was thankfully willing to get involved.

Things were looking good and they were ready to go when John looked at the case file over Christmas and realised they hadn't followed up on the 999 call, so he went ahead and requested it. It was this request which brought on the delay in the trial as it took time for the 999 call to be admitted into evidence. The judge wasn't pleased but granted the extension all the same. This was a blessing in disguise as the 999 call became a highly crucial piece of evidence to back up my version of events while also letting the jury hear just how distressed I was. The team of police canvassed the area looking for witnesses to strengthen our case and came upon the previous burglary in my street and managed to charge Him with that as well as the charges in my case. As He had pleaded guilty to that burglary, He would be sentenced for that at the same time as being sentenced for the burglary and theft in my flat. He had come up against this judge before and John felt confident that if found guilty the judge wouldn't be too lenient in sentencing.

John felt we had presented a strong case to the judge and jury, and he was hopeful they would make the right decision. Everyone had questions for John, and before we knew it, it was past five o'clock. The jury was excused for the night to continue their deliberations in the morning, and we headed back to the hotel for another night of surmising about the verdict.

John had given us hope that everything would work out but as the evening wore on doubt crept in amongst us. My father was adamant he didn't care one way or the other and I genuinely believed he didn't. He was just relieved to get it over with. All he wanted now was to get home and put it all behind us. My mother was going to be totally crushed if a not-guilty verdict was returned because she was convinced the jury saw Him for what He was. I, on the other hand, was unsure about what exactly lay ahead. I was too terrified to be hopeful and too tired to discuss it or worry about it any longer.

Friday morning was a mixture of nerves and anticipation. Everyone knew that one way or another it would be over today and this brought us all some comfort. 'Bring it on!' I said to everyone on the tube, 'I can't cope with the waiting anymore.' I'm sure that was more than evident. We got to the courthouse and went back to the waiting room. The tension while we waited was unbearable and we could do nothing but sit in silence. All I wanted was a cigarette but I couldn't be bothered with the drama of going through security and back again. I was also terrified that the second I moved they would have reached a decision.

It was after eleven when John came in to tell us the jury had reached their verdict and we could make our way back into the courtroom. 'Oh, Jesus Christ,' I said. I was asked where I wanted to sit. I hadn't thought about it but decided to sit with my parents, not considering how it would make Phil feel. I feel bad about that now, but I don't regret it. We filed into the courtroom and I sat between my parents, directly opposite Him. My supporters filled the seats as everyone in our party made their way into the courtroom for the first time that week. I still couldn't bring myself to look at Him, deciding to look instead at the jury. I was terrified none of them would look back at me, and I had convinced myself it would be a not-guilty verdict. I was visibly shaking, and my dad asked me if I was all right. 'Honestly, no. I think I'm going to be sick,' I answered. I could taste the bile at the back of my throat and could hardly swallow the water in my mouth.

'Do not be sick,' my mother said. 'Not now.'

The judge asked us to stand. He could hardly be bothered to get up from His seat. The judge asked the foreman if they had reached a verdict.

He responded, 'We have, Your Honour.'

'How do you find the defendant on the charge of rape?'

'We find the defendant *guilty*, Your Honour.'

The foreman was trying his hardest not to cry, and suddenly there was a collective 'YES!' from our side of the room. I burst out crying along with my supporters, Julie and quite a few members of the jury. The judge gave us a few moments to collect ourselves and I buried my head in my daddy's chest crying uncontrollably. I wasn't ashamed of my tears this time. I forced myself to look at Him for the first time all week and I was genuinely surprised to discover He looked shocked and pale at the verdict. I wanted to laugh at Him and His stupidity in thinking He could get away with it. I got you, you motherfucker. You're not fucking smiling or winking at my mother now, are you, you lying, cowardly, low-down piece of crap.

He hung His head and His wife started shouting, 'You keep your head up. You've done nothing wrong, baby. It's her fault and she wanted some black cock anyway!' I couldn't believe it. After everything, I couldn't believe she uttered those words. Her comments stopped everyone in their tracks. The judge banged on his gavel asking for order in the courtroom. Security appeared and created a barrier between them and us. Nobody on my side had uttered a sound, and I was too gobsmacked to even think of responding to her. It was further evidence she shouldn't be allowed to bring up children with an attitude like that. Maybe she came from the same planet as Him and they were dark soulmates who revelled in their life of crime. How they found each other, I would never understand. Either way, they should have come with a hazard warning visible to all normal people that said, 'Caution: risk of serious injury. Approach with extreme care – bits missing on the inside.'

His barrister jumped in with a request to delay sentencing so she could prepare reports on His behalf. The judge denied her request saying that sentencing would take place after lunch, at two. He was removed first with His wife and family escorted out after. It was then we broke our silence cheering, hugging, crying and kissing each other. It was truly one of the most emotional scenes I've ever been part of and I'll never forget it or how we all felt for as long as I live. We sat outside a cafe across the road, all of us at a big table, and I had a sandwich and crisps – the first bit of solid food I'd eaten all week, but I could hardly enjoy it for laughing. I laughed and laughed and laughed and laughed some more. I was overjoyed at the turn of events. I was euphoric, and eternally grateful to the members of the jury who had recognised the truth. I felt vindicated. I phoned Judy and when she phoned me back I couldn't hear her for the cheers and whoops from everybody. I told her He was being sentenced in the afternoon and she told me to enjoy my day. I was going to enjoy every minute of it for I had earned it. We headed back to the courtroom for sentencing. I had prepared myself for it to be somewhere between five and seven years, I had to be realistic about these things, but I quietly prayed and asked God for more.

Chapter Seventeen

The judge informed us we would hear from His barrister first, and security was present in case the maniac wife started ranting again. I noticed the presence of other barristers not involved in the case – it seemed my barrister had caught the interest of her fellow professionals with her win in a rape case and they were here for the sentencing, it being high profile. I was nervous but not nausea nervous.

I sat between my parents again and listened to His barrister explain that His life of crime was perpetrated by an addiction to drugs which He had tried desperately to curb. He had been to rehab on more than one occasion while in prison but had fallen off the wagon on His return to the streets. She went on to explain how He was needed at home to provide for His wife and children. She actually went far enough to say that He was a, and I quote, 'a family man at heart.' I thought my father was going to blow a gasket at that suggestion, and rightly so. My father is a family man and this description of Him was one step too far. Daddy was shaking with anger at the suggestion they might have anything in common. I put my arm around him and told him it was all right.

The judge said he'd heard enough and He was to be removed from the courtroom for my witness impact statement to be read out to the jury. I was unprepared for just how depressing my life sounded when my barrister read out the statement, and most of the jury and my supporters were crying throughout the speech. It was a true account of my daily activities and showed just how hard normal, everyday tasks had become for me. I guess it spelled out the difficulties Phil and I were having as well and this was extremely upsetting for both of us. While it was important for the court to understand my predicament, it was another step over the line of what was personal to Phil and myself, and I begrudged sharing it with everyone. I made it clear I had lost my career as well as everything else because I was never going to return to London to work and there were no services for children requiring a bone marrow transplant in Northern Ireland. At the end of the statement I said that the events of that day had pressed pause on my life and I was still waiting for someone to press play so I could begin to move forward.

That time had finally arrived when He was brought back into the courtroom and told to stand up for sentencing. The judge gave a little speech about how heinous a crime it was to commit burglary and theft, never mind rape and false imprisonment. The judge made it clear that he believed His threats to kill me had been unnecessary and that He should also have been charged with aggravated robbery and aggravated assault which carried a longer prison sentence. The whole situation was made more traumatic by Him making me relive my experience in court, which I could have been spared had He pleaded guilty to the crimes He had committed. The judge was heartfelt in his words and seemed genuinely distressed for me.

It was time for sentencing. Everyone continued crying quietly, especially me. I made myself look at Him again. I wanted the last image of Him in my head to be His expression when He was sentenced and not what He did to me in my own home. For the crime of burglary, He was sentenced to eight years in prison. He was sentenced to two years for each of the six counts of attempted theft and two years for each count of actual theft, which amounted to another four years, and He was sentenced to another two years on the separate burglary charge. These sentences were to run concurrently, which I didn't understand at the time but which John later explained meant they ran at the same time. So we were basically looking at eight years of prison time in total so far. On the charge of rape, the judge sentenced Him to *life* in prison, to serve a minimum time of fifteen years. You heard everyone's short intake of breath and gasp of shock until there was complete silence in the courtroom. He looked fairly shocked Himself and seemed to sway where He was standing. This time I didn't feel like laughing and continued to cry. They were tears of relief that it was over and tears of relief that He would never again come upon a young woman, alone, in her own home. They were also tears for that young woman I would never be again. Finally, I had done what I could to put it right and put Him where He belonged. When the judge asked them to take Him down, He looked at His wife who continued to tell Him to hold His head up high and that He'd done nothing wrong. She continued to shout abuse at me as she was led out of the courtroom.

The judge thanked the police who had worked so hard and presented the case so well. He thanked the barristers and he thanked the jury for their time and in coming to the correct conclusion. The judge then addressed me directly, thanking me for giving evidence and praising me for being one of bravest and most courageous witnesses he had ever had in his courtroom. He thanked my family and friends for the graceful way in which they had conducted themselves in what must have been an extremely difficult week. He fervently hoped that the conclusion of the case in the legal sense of the word would let me move on, and he sincerely hoped we had pressed play so my life could begin again.

—⁓⁓∽∽∽⁓⁓—

To say we were emotional could never begin to describe the feelings everyone had on Friday afternoon. We filed out of the courtroom and made our way back to the hotel, meeting members of the jury en route. We weren't allowed to talk to them but my father thanked them on the way past for we were truly indebted to each of them. We went to the hotel bar and, God, was I ready for a drink. The police team came with us and most of my lovely friends from work stopped by to join in the celebrations. There was a large crowd and it didn't take long before we were drunk on the wine due to the very little sleep and food consumed all week. It was one of the most magical evenings I've ever had and I loved every minute of it.

Anne and my parents left for the airport while my friends and I continued to party – we weren't leaving until Saturday morning. I had a quiet word with John voicing my concerns for His children and he told me the police had already been in touch with social services. Last year there was a domestic incident charge brought against Him when He tried to kill His wife and there were concerns regarding the nature of His relationship with His teenage stepdaughter which required further investigation. His wife had later dropped the charges and without her evidence there was no case. The same wife who had so valiantly defended Him in court and said that I had wanted some 'black cock', thereby admitting she knew it to be true but had chosen to believe it was somehow my fault and not His. Satisfied the police were dealing with it, I told John I didn't want to know any more as I was about to lose all my lovely wine.

We drank and drank until we could drink no more and then went for Chinese food. The atmosphere was electric and everyone was on top of the world. I could hardly get my fork to my mouth I was so tired and decided to call it a night in the hope of not being totally hungover for my flight in the morning. Phil was flying with me as he too was totally shattered and needed a break, and I couldn't wait to see the 'Welcome to Belfast' sign. I slept well that night, fuelled by the wine, and was delighted to be going home and excited to see everyone and share the good news.

We didn't do much over the next few weeks except relax. We went for long walks with Charlie Brown and hung about my parents' house. Loads of people called in and we discussed our legal victory repeatedly. I was continually congratulated on doing so well but was very conscious it had been a team effort. Phil and I were so tired and a little bit withdrawn, both still reeling from the intrusion into our private life. There was nothing sacred in my life any more, everyone knew every detail of me on the inside and the out as if they had examined every cell in my body, held me under a microscope and inspected everything about my life and were dismayed to find it wasn't perfect. Again, like I was lacking in something or missing something that was important.

The time came for Phil to return to London and his normal life. I wish I could tell you there's a happy ending for us, that we managed to get through it together, but I can't. I wish I could tell you we found each other again but we didn't. I wish I could tell you He didn't break us, but He most certainly did. Most of all I wish I could tell you we managed to stay friends and support each other in our recovery but we aren't and we didn't. We couldn't. The darkness had settled in around us and between us and it was just too much; It was just too terrible. We ended our relationship over the phone shortly after Phil returned to London. We talked initially and tried to stay in touch but it was difficult and painful and reminded us of the awfulness of it all and we gradually stopped talking and let each other go.

The euphoria of the verdict wore off over the next few weeks. I was very sad about Phil and me and was having trouble sleeping again. The nightmares had resumed full throttle and I realised the verdict hadn't changed anything for me – I was still left with the awfulness of it all in my head and body and I was very quietly panicking at how I would cope with the awfulness of it all alone. At least Phil had been there and knew everything, which went some way to sharing it with me. I felt sure I would never be in another relationship again and was doomed to be a singleton forever.

I felt an incredible amount of pressure to be chirpy and upbeat about everything but I was closer to the edge than ever before. My driving test was just around the corner and I had forgotten how to reverse, parallel park and do a three-point turn. I had serious decisions to make about my future that I had put to one side while focusing on the trial, but now it was over I had no choice but to think about those things and make some decisions. What was I going to do for a job? How was I going to pay my bills? How long would I live with my parents? When would I have enough energy to care about those issues and sit down and give them serious thought? I spent a lot of time in the vacant place in my head beneath the security of my sunglasses and generally avoided any well-meaning discussions about my future. My mother tried her best to engage me but I refused to be drawn. I wanted to give my head and body time to get over the trial and get with the programme.

It was a seriously bad omen when I realised my driving test was on a Tuesday. After sixty-two lessons everyone was sure I would pass but I knew different. Being in the car with a strange man terrified me though I knew that was irrational, but, hey, stranger things had happened and after The Terrible Tuesday I believed everyone had the capacity to hurt me. However, I had to do it. Unfortunately it was much worse than I thought it would be. My legs shook so much I could hardly push the clutch in and I stalled the car before I'd even left the test centre. My instructor was surprised I'd failed and simply put it down to a bad day, but I knew at this rate I was never going to pass the bloody thing.

I'd decided to resign from work. I was never going to live or work in London and there was no point putting it off any longer. I was devastated leaving my career behind as well as everything else and felt such deep sadness at resigning that I didn't think I could cope with going over and saying goodbye to everyone properly. It wasn't what they deserved; they had been so supportive since that day and I had many good friends who deserved a decent goodbye but didn't get one.

I posted my letter and they sent me a beautiful leaving present and a great card. It was with a heavy heart that I accepted my career was finished and I would have to start over at home. In what area of children's nursing, I had no idea, but I had to do something as I was totally and utterly broke. Phil and I had bought a house together before The Terrible Tuesday and I had to buy him out of it. We had borrowed the deposit from his dad and I had him to pay back too. I had to make the mortgage payments by myself and I had no money, no job and already owed my brother-in-law and parents a fortune.

My solicitor friend had filled in the forms for compensation from the government and sent me to a psychiatrist for an assessment as part of the claim. The psychiatrist's report nearly sent me over the edge entirely with catchphrases like 'severe post-traumatic disorder' – I always think when something's a disorder you're a bit fucked from the outset. He talked about anxiety, stress, depression, flashbacks and severe panic attacks, and about how I might never fully recover. Oh God, but that report depressed me, and Judy was angry at me reading it. Never once had she mentioned post-traumatic stress disorder – having never focused on labelling how I felt or where I was at. Thank God for Judy. I was depressed reading it, anxious and paranoid of my thoughts and feelings, trying to work out what a flashback was and how bad my panic attacks were. I had no idea just how bad I looked on paper and tried to believe Judy when she told me it was just a report and not a true reflection of me or how I was doing.

Chapter Eighteen

The two months after the trial were the worst since The Terrible Tuesday. Everything was so messed up. I had no direction and no idea what I was going to do with my life or what I was capable of doing. Judy and I took up our shamanic work again asking for guidance in every aspect of my life: my hyper anxiety and inability to sleep, my emotions and mood swings, my career and job prospects and my financial situation. Each one was as bad as the other and I seriously thought things were never going to improve for me. I had agreed to give Him one year but I feared He was going to take much more than that if I let Him. I just couldn't seem to move forward. There were days I could hardly speak, much less get showered or dressed, and there were nights I never went to bed just so I didn't have to face the horror of bedtime. Then there were days of boundless energy and days of extreme anger. My mother appeared some mornings to find the contents of the kitchen, the bathroom or the utility room on the floor and I would declare that her house was disgusting and I didn't know how she lived in it as I bleached everything to within an inch of its life.

Other days I made enough food for about thirty people making a complete mess in her kitchen. 'Who is going to eat that?' she would say. I hadn't thought of who would eat it and we would have to share it out amongst my siblings. The two things my mother hates the smell of are garlic and bleach, and I used both in abundance with no thought whatsoever for her. I drove her mental. No matter what sort of a nutjob I'd been or what had occurred during the day, she would make me supper at night and stay with me as long as she could before she went to bed leaving me to my night-time horrors.

Judy said maybe I was trying to do too much at once, so we broke it down with the first thing being the driving. I went for another test and told the examiner I was very nervous – not about the driving but being in the car with him. I told him I was going to vomit during the parallel park and asked him if I would fail if I got out of the car for a minute. He said I wouldn't fail and that there was nothing to be nervous of. He must have felt so sorry for me, and even though I parked in a bus lane he passed me anyway. The best thing about it was that it was on a Tuesday and I could give The Terrible Tuesday a big *fuck you.*

I took the car to my next counselling session leaving home an hour before my appointment. I arrived sweating and terrified, it having taken me forty minutes to park the car. I seriously considered leaving it there and walking home. Despite my anxiety I knew driving gave me a bit of independence to take Charlie Brown away for longer, nicer walks and to go places on my own. It also meant I could apply for a job at the local hospital, a forty-minute drive from my parents' house. As it happened, they didn't have any job vacancies but there was a job in community nursing. It was a secondment to do a degree in community and public health nursing at the same time as working. I'd enjoyed my community placements as a student and felt this was something I could do.

The pace was much slower than I was used to but it meant more time with patients and therefore delivery of a higher standard of care within a home setting. I applied and got an interview. The only stumbling block was I was a nervous wreck and didn't think I could handle an interview. Also, inevitably they would ask about my sick leave from work, and I didn't think I could talk about it in an interview, so Judy and I discussed it and decided the best way forward was to tell them it was personal and that I would discuss it with my potential boss. I would simply give that person a newspaper article about it which meant I wouldn't have to say too much.

I went for the interview weighed down with healing crystals. As it turned out, I knew the lead nurse who was interviewing me. She was my potential boss and had been one of my mentors when I was a student. When it came to the questions on my sick leave, I asked to speak to her privately. We went outside, even though she said she felt it was inappropriate. When I gave her the article she said, 'Oh, Jesus Christ!' and asked me to give her a minute before we carried on with the interview.

I wasn't sure how it had went but I got a telephone call that night to tell me I'd been successful, and she said she understood how difficult it would have been to discuss my sick leave with strangers. The job and the degree started in September, so I was officially out of work and money until then. I didn't know how I would handle starting a new job, never mind travelling to Belfast and meeting new people or studying on top of all that, but I had a few months before I had to worry about it, and I had no choice – I had to give it a go.

It was coming up to the first anniversary of The Terrible Tuesday. I had magnified it in my head to mean something, and it was important not to have a complete breakdown before this date because if I made it through the first year then my chances of having a complete breakdown were smaller. But it was difficult to know how long you could stand on the edge without falling off, and sometimes I thought I should just save myself the hassle of waiting for the edge to catch me and just jump. It couldn't have been much worse than where my head was anyway, and, you know, maybe sanity is overrated. Maybe I'd already had a complete breakdown and no one had told me about it – it would have just given me something else to worry about.

That was three things I could strike off my list and that had to count as progress. I could drive, I had a car (courtesy of my father) and I was starting a new job in a few months. The next thing was living arrangements. I couldn't live with my parents forever, much as I wanted to. The house Phil and I had bought was in the process of becoming my house and would be ready for me to move into in July. The thought of leaving my parents was excruciating but I knew if I didn't do it soon, I'd never do it. I had a small window of opportunity that I had to grab with both hands. If I rented the house to someone else, it would be at least another year before I could move in, so I said I would move in mid-July and at least I had Charlie Brown to protect me. My brother only lived across the lane, so him and his wife would always be nearby if anything was wrong or if I needed anything. Strike number four.

My English friends were coming over for the first anniversary, and after this one I would never officially mark the anniversary again, but we needed to celebrate this one. I had lost a lot over the past twelve months but I hadn't lost my mind, not entirely anyway, and that was worth celebrating. They were all staying with my parents and my mother made us all lunch. We stayed at the dining room table and drank champagne and smoked all day. We laughed so much, we drank so much and we smoked so much that we laughed some more. We laughed until we cried and some of the time we cried too. Then we laughed again.

That day was such a turning point for me. It was the day I decided to be grateful. To be grateful I was at my dining room table drinking champagne and smoking with my friends. I had agreed to give Him one year of my life and I had kept my end of the bargain. I tried not to be too sad at what I had lost over the last twelve months and stopped myself from compiling a list of the lost things in my head. It was a bonus I could drive, that I had a house to move into and a job to start. I took comfort in the knowledge that never again would He hurt another woman, at least not for the next twenty years, which is not forever but it would have to do. I knew The Terrible Tuesday had changed me but I hoped to use it to lead the sort of life I wanted to lead, to do the sorts of things I wanted to do and to spend my time how I chose to. I was a much quieter person, a lot less opinionated and judgemental of people than I used to be. I thought before I spoke. I could appreciate hardship on a deeper level than before and that would benefit me in the years to come. I hoped I wouldn't just join the rat race in September when I started my new job. I had had a massive wake-up call and I didn't want the universe to give me another one.

I was reminded of Judy's phrase: central focus. I tried to be honest when I asked myself if it still had a central focus in my life. The answer was, yes, of course it had central focus. It controlled my every waking minute and I didn't know if that would ever change. It controlled most of my sleeping as well unless I was drunk or on sleeping pills, and I didn't know if that would ever change either. I knew, however, that I would never give up trying to change that. I would never give up the quest for peace in my head, my heart, my body and my soul. I would do whatever it took to move it from centre stage and I didn't care how long it took. I would never give up because if I gave up I would be giving it to Him and I wouldn't willingly give Him another second of my time.

So I just had to do it: move house, go to work, drive to Belfast and study for my degree. I would have to think about meeting someone new but it was enough to focus on getting comfortable with my new arrangements first. It was there for the long haul and I had to make room for it, get used to it and start moving around it and past it.

PART THREE
The Recovery

When a big change occurs in your life it forces you to change direction. Sometimes the new path may not be easy, but you can be absolutely certain that there is magnificence for you on the new path. You can be absolutely certain that the new path contains things that you would not have experienced otherwise. When we look back at a negative event that occurred in the past, we often see how in fact it transformed our life. We see how that event directed us towards a life that we would not change for anything.

The Secret
Daily Teachings – Tuesday
Day 240

Chapter Nineteen

It didn't take long for July to roll round and for the house to be ready to be made a home. I spent a couple of weeks painting, my dad bought me some furniture and then it was time to move in. Despite being totally broke and my dad paying, on top of everything else, the mortgage too, it was now or never. I moved my belongings out gradually until one day my mum and sister brought all my stuff from my parents' house in one go. There was no excuse to delay any longer. The house was secured like Fort Knox, I had Charlie Brown and my brother was across the lane if I needed anything. How bad could it be, right?

Excruciating. In the beginning every little noise had me out of bed in a flash and every time the dog made a sound I dashed around the house like a lunatic. At every slight movement I checked the locks on the windows and the doors, turned the lights on and off so whoever was outside would know someone was awake inside the house. Every one of my senses was on high alert and I couldn't relax enough to get any sleep. The temptation to move back to my parents' was overwhelming but I knew if I didn't stick it out I would be living with them forever, and I refused to be limited in my ability to live a normal life.

One of my friends was living with her parents and it was decided that she would move in with me – at the very least we would be company for each other. Unfortunately it was short-lived. At home with her family she would regularly get locked out and had to climb in a window to avoid waking anyone. While staying with me she went out one Saturday night, lost her keys and, naturally enough in a slightly drunken haze, tried to climb in through the kitchen window. I was in bed when the dog barked but thankfully my sister was staying over that night and we both got up to see what the commotion was. All I could see walking through the kitchen door was one long leg coming in the window. I remember thinking, 'This cannot be happening to me, seriously not happening. Not again.' I didn't put it together that it was only her and that it was okay, nothing bad was going to happen. The dog, meanwhile, was about to eat her alive and in the confusion of it all I nearly passed out in the kitchen. My sister told me to wait in the bedroom and when I reached it I just collapsed in a heap on the floor.

I had a serious panic attack: I was green, couldn't breathe and was hyperventilating. Charlie Brown was lying on top of me trying to protect me, but the loving gesture made it even more difficult to breathe properly, and I couldn't find my voice to call my sister to come in and move the damn dog. I couldn't calm down and couldn't be cajoled back to bed in my own house. I had gone to the vacant place in my head and could hardly utter a coherent sentence – something my sister found hard to handle. Eventually she phoned our mother who collected us and took us back to our parents' house. Things didn't seem so bad in the light of day, however. I knew I had to return to the house and give it another go – I couldn't give up, but it was a sharp reminder of just how little could send me careering over the edge into oblivion. It scared me and I was so angry it had happened – not angry at her per se, it was what she was used to doing and when you're drunk you don't think straight. It was a big wake-up call for us though and she moved out before living together ruined our friendship altogether.

In the end she probably got a lucky break. There were days I was fine during that first summer – everything was A-okay. Then came days of acute fear and panic when I cleaned obsessively and couldn't get rid of the knots in my stomach or the panicky feeling in my chest never mind the exhaustion from only getting a couple hours sleep at a time.

Quite early on in my new abode, a man came to the kitchen window for directions. He couldn't quite believe I didn't know where he was looking for, so he got a bit irritated and aggressive – so much so I nearly passed out in the kitchen; my legs went to jelly and I had to hold onto the worktop to stop from falling in a heap. I held my breath for so long that the room started spinning and I had to lie with my face on the cold kitchen tiles until I felt semi-normal again.

At times like these I thought I'd never make it – that I would never be able to live on my own or feel comfortable or confident in the house by myself. It was difficult to relax and have faith that everything would be okay, that bad things didn't have to happen. I was plagued with nightmares when I did manage sleep and would wake crying, sweating and shaking until I could turn all the lights on and make a cup of tea and smoke cigarettes. I was actually looking forward to starting work and getting my degree underway just to get out of the house. I hoped I would be so tired by it all that I would find it easier to sleep.

———∿∿◦◦◦◦◦◦∿∿———

My boss was a truly lovely woman who gave me time to go to my counselling appointments. She was very sympathetic to my situation and my recovery which I greatly appreciated. When I started work the community team were in the throes of moving to the old children's ward at the local hospital. The office was a large, open space which was lovely but had only one entry and exit. There was a continual stream of workmen coming and going – painting, moving things, fixing lights, setting up computers and whatnot. It practically gave me a nervous breakdown trying to get past them to leave the office. My stress levels were fried by it all, so I went out on home visits as much as possible. This too was nerve-racking as I was driving on roads I didn't know and going into strangers' houses by myself. Every visit and every road was a potentially dangerous situation where I could get hurt. I was undeniably terrified of it all.

My boss got me a mobile phone and we started a diary of where I was going and what time I was due back so someone knew where I was at all times. She must have felt like my mother but these small changes brought me great comfort and let me do my job with confidence. However, there were some occasions I just couldn't face it – the office or out on visits. Those days she let me work from home as long as she could contact me any time. I kept education boards, did research and always showed her what I was doing so she knew I wasn't taking the piss. I tried to do a good job but it was a relief to start my degree and only be in the office two days a week.

Getting to Belfast was harder than I thought. My brain wasn't in great working order and I had lost the ability to multitask. I found driving nerve-racking, what with all the lane changing, the motorway, merging traffic and thousands of bloody roundabouts. I would eventually arrive at my destination exhausted, shaky and wondering how I was going to make it back home. Thankfully I befriended a lovely girl from a neighbouring county who was doing the same course as me. From then on I drove to her house and she drove us the rest of the way. If it wasn't for her I probably wouldn't have made it at all.

I hadn't thought how hard it would be to study again, and my lack of concentration for any length of time surprised me. I couldn't read a book or watch a movie because half an hour into anything I would be walking about or thinking about something else. I sometimes went to the vacant place in my head and thought about nothing at all. My brain just couldn't do it; it was too taxing and I convinced myself I would never get through it. My new friend was a great source of support along with another girl I met, someone I had done my diploma with years before. I gave the two of them an overview of what had happened, explained I was a bit of a basket case and was unsure if I could do the degree at all. They were both horrified but were so helpful throughout the course. I passed my modules okay until it came to the one on child protection. It was then I had a mini-meltdown.

The police talked to us about actual cases of child abuse and showed us authentic photographs of abused children. They told us horrendous stories of some awful things that happen to children every fucking day of the week. All I wanted to do was get up and leave but I was glued to the chair. It was one of the first times I had thought of it happening to other people, and thinking of it happening to children wasn't a good place to start. That sounds unbelievable but I lived inside my own head and didn't entertain thoughts of what other people went through.

My mother vetoed all my television and reading materials. She would say, 'Don't watch that programme on BBC 1 tonight at nine, it's not suitable for you,' or, 'Don't read that new Michael Connelly book, it's not suitable for you.' Therefore, I rarely turned on the television or read anything. The shock of it all was harrowing. I shook and could taste bile at the back of my throat. I was utterly distraught at the idea of being sexually abused by someone you loved. Being abused by a stranger is bad enough but by someone you love must be unbearable. I was conscious I had a lot to be thankful for in my own situation. At least I was a fully functioning adult who understood that rape is about violence and control and nothing to do with love or expressing love for another person. I had experienced love in a healthy way and had a loving relationship with my family. I was old enough to understand how wrong it was to do that to another human being. At least it was not an everyday occurrence for me. How the fuck children got through that I had no clue. The thought of it scared me and sent me over the edge again in my head. I fell off the recovery wagon and was a complete wreck. A friend was planning her wedding, she needed me to be a good friend and I didn't support her in the way she had supported me. Instead, I stopped going to university or doing anything for a couple of weeks.

The pressure of the course, the job and being so completely broke got to me and I felt my head was going to explode. It was nearly a year since the trial and I thought of everything in terms of a court of law – how my life would look if inspected under a microscope again. I continuously dreamt of the trial and of giving evidence over and over again. Judy told me it was my body's way of remembering but it made it no less unpleasant, the physical reminders of trial week. The nightmares, flashbacks, panic attacks, the anxiety, insomnia and the continual smoking left me looking like I'd been dragged through a hedge backwards rendering me unable to get dressed some days. I was juggling ten different balls in the air always terrified they were about to fall down round me bringing everything else in my life crashing down with them.

———————

Judy and I scheduled an extra appointment to take up our shamanic work again to give me some strength and guidance as I still had to discuss the challenges of daily living with her so I could find ways to move around them and move forward. I wasn't the only one having a hard time dealing with the reminders of trial week. I'd been in touch with Phil who was having a hard time with it too. My heart went out to him for he had his own recovery ahead of him and it was a difficult road to be on.

My friends were in a similar situation with the anniversary of the trial looming. Everyone was having trouble sleeping, having nightmares and remembering what a difficult week it was. Finally, it arrived. Having anticipated the insomnia, I'd booked the week off work. I slept in, drank wine with the chicks, took the dog for lovely walks, and before I knew it, it had been and gone. My head settled down a bit once the first anniversary of the trial passed, and I mustered up the courage to go back to university and work. I was committed to finishing the bloody degree although I knew I was in serious need of assistance if I was to see it through to the end.

Chapter Twenty

Judy and I started journeying again. First we decided on an intention, usually that I was journeying to the lower world to meet my power animal to ask for help with everyday life or help with my emotions. My primary concern was to get help with my sleeping and my anger. I was mildly irritated all the time and was irrationally angry over small things, but couldn't control my feelings even while being aware of how irrational they were. I verbalised my journey, which was quite hard to do, and Judy recorded it. Then we listened to the recording and discussed my journey — the messages that came through and how I would apply them to daily life. Sometimes I met Cat and we headed to the upper world; on rare occasions I had a middle world journey.

My first few journeys were always the same no matter my intention. I would find the tree, make my way down the tunnel and come out at a clearing in a forest-type area. I would meet Cat who would take off into the night and I would clamber after her until we came to the edge of a very dark, scary wood. I could hear the trees rustling in the wind but couldn't see in front of me. There was no other way round the wood except to go through it.

Cat would go in despite me begging her not to. I would be terrified, totally terrified and unable to breathe with a knot the size of Brazil in my stomach. The wood was so dark and menacing it always left me with a bad vibe. Something wasn't quite right and I could feel it. I knew there was a dark hooded figure in the middle of it and I knew I would eventually have to make my way in, but at the beginning I did everything possible not to. I hid behind trees and tried to quiet my breathing so he wouldn't find me. I willed Cat not to go any further but she would just mosey on through the wood, plonk herself down in the middle of the trees and wait for me to catch up. It was so frustrating to journey and always end up there. I wanted to cancel my appointments and back out of shamanic work entirely but I just couldn't. I knew Judy would be disappointed and I couldn't do that to her. At least, not willingly.

What did I have to lose? On my next journey I decided to walk through the woods and sit down next to Cat. It was pitch black, yet I knew my way around. I saw the hooded figure and I said hello. I sat down and refused to give in to the fear in my belly or make a run for it. I sat long enough to stop my breathing coming in short, shallow, panicky gasps and long enough to even relax the knot in my stomach. Eventually Cat got up and made her way through the trees towards a bridge. We crossed over and were met with sunshine and light at the other side of the woods. We did this over and over again, Cat and I, until I was no longer afraid of the passage through the woods.

Through our discussions I concluded I was journeying inside myself and the wood was a place of my own making; a place I held all the fear, horror and the darkness from The Terrible Tuesday which manifested itself in my head, my chest and in a big ball in my belly. I was continually looking for a way to go around it but that wasn't going to happen – it wasn't how these things worked. I had to accept it was there and I had to get comfortable with it. I had to learn not to be afraid of it if I was going to get through it and out the other side – and I definitely didn't want to get stuck in the middle of it. Getting stuck in the wood would be like watching the scary part of a film on repeat and never getting to the end where the good guy usually came out the winner.

If I let the darkness inside my head, my chest and my belly take control, it would only be a matter of time before I no longer cared about myself or other people. It would only be a matter of time before I could do terrible things to myself or other people too. I couldn't let that happen.

I'd listened to a song about suicide quite a bit and I'd come to view it as a viable option in particularly dark moments. I hadn't made any plans but I'd been thinking about it and sometimes, especially at night, it popped into my head as something I should give a bit of thought to – just putting myself out of my own fucking misery and giving up the fight. In the calming light of day I realised how stupid it was to have that thought stuck in my head; that my mother would never forgive me if I took that road of darkness and that she would probably hound me to the realms of hell and back for putting her through it. She assured me throughout my Roman Catholic upbringing that taking your own life was unforgivable in the eyes of God and I would indeed go straight to hell. I didn't necessarily believe that statement, for God is meant to forgive all sin if you repent, but that too confused me. Surely suicide is no greater a sin than rape or murder? The people who commit those vile acts are told to repent and seek forgiveness, and if the big man upstairs can forgive those evil acts, then surely he can forgive a desperate person who kills themself when they just couldn't put up with their insides any more.

The problem with my theory, however, is that I wasn't sure what would happen when I died. No one could be one hundred per cent sure what happened or where we go, so I decided it wasn't worth the risk. What if I went straight to hell and hell *was* the living place of every dark thing? I'd have to spend my days in darkness instead of spending them here where there are at least a few hours of light. After much debate I'd ruled out suicide as a potential option. I wouldn't allow myself to think of it any more and I wouldn't give it room to manifest through the fear within me. It was maybe just another example of how much control the darkness had over me at times. Suicide is a seriously dark thought and I was the only person who had the power to stop thinking about it.

Journeying into the woods and becoming more comfortable with the darkness and not giving in to my fear made me feel more in control of my emotions. I was a tad more in control of my own anxiety, my own stress levels and I was giving them less and less power to scare the living crap out of me daily. It was uplifting to manage even small periods of time when I wasn't terrified of everything and everyone. Eventually the hooded figure didn't even bother showing up in the woods, and I theorised that he fed solely on my fear and if I wasn't afraid then the game was no longer fun for him – he was only interested in playing if he was going to win all the time and I had had enough of being beaten.

I took this message into my everyday life and realised I had to stop being afraid. I had to stop being afraid of everyone and every situation I found myself in. I had to remember that not everyone was out to hurt me. I knew there were people in the world filled with darkness who did terrible things, but I also knew there were people who weren't filled with darkness and who didn't do terrible things to each other. I decided to have a little faith in the general population, to be reasonable with myself and in my thinking.

When I next journeyed I found myself back at the house where I met the Egyptian woman before the trial. It was here I found myself and got the strength to face Him at the trial. On a symbolic level that house was in fact my house. That house was the place I held my memories and past experiences and the place where I'd lost parts of myself; however, it was also the place I could find them again. It was huge, with lots of levels and lots of rooms. On one particular journey I found a young woman sitting on a large bed in one of those huge rooms waiting for me. She was scared, alone and couldn't leave the bed. I immediately knew she was a part of me – I left her there on the morning of The Terrible Tuesday when I was terrified and alone on my own bed in my flat. I was certain this abandonment happened when the light went out behind my eyes and in my head.

In that journey, I took the woman downstairs with me. She was so afraid but I held her hand and gently told her it was okay and that she couldn't stay there forever, that I didn't want her to stay there forever, so I took her outside into the garden. When she realised she was free of the bedroom and of the fear she started to dance and jump around with joy. She was so relieved to be outside and breathing fresh air. I just stood there watching her. That was another significant part of my recovery. It was another part of the healing process for me, and I let go of some of the fear I had held onto since that day. I was making progress and moving in the right direction.

I was aware this all sounded quite strange if you'd never encountered shamanism but I could only tell you that journeying to a different reality gave me the freedom inside my head to let go of some of the horror of The Terrible Tuesday and to move to a place beyond the horror and the fear that threatened to overwhelm me and keep me a hostage to the awfulness of it forever. It's described as a journey of deep personal, spiritual growth, and I'm testament to the truth of that description.

Yet again I felt a shift of something on the inside. I was more centred, more focused and more determined to beat the darkness. More than anything I was stronger than I was three months ago. I wouldn't let this have centre stage in my life forever. I'd almost come to the end of my degree and had been offered a temporary contract with the community nursing team once it was finished. I was relieved I'd have a job and be able to pay my own mortgage. I was trying hard to relax the inside of my head and belly, and I was getting better at being in my house by myself. I was more relaxed meeting strangers and less panicky about every situation I found myself in. I had grown more comfortable in my new life and grown very close to my brother and his wife across the lane. He rarely turned his lights out or went to bed before I did. His very presence reassured me every time I looked out the window, and although the responsibility of living so close to me must have lay heavily on him, he never said a word. His wife worked from home and was always around during the day, so I was rarely ever alone. I was truly grateful for the security and companionship they gave me on a daily basis. I wasn't sure if I would feel so secure if they weren't across the road, and I sincerely hoped to God they never moved house in case I had to move with them.

Through my journeying I was guided towards meditation. I met a lovely spirit guide called Jay who explained the process and showed me how to meditate. I wanted to just sit comfortably on my own, close my eyes and concentrate on my breathing. On this journey through life we are aided by the elements of the earth and everything is connected on an energetic level. I'm aware that we all have an aura, an energetic field, and that we have certain energy points throughout our bodies called the chakra system. Jay told me to imagine I was accessing the energy of the earth, and through every breath I took I was bringing the energy up through the soles of my feet through every energy point in my body. He told me to see it in my mind, with my mind's eye or my third eye, and to feel it coming up through my body and relaxing every part of me.

Some days, unsurprisingly, I couldn't relax enough to focus, but I knew, like most things, it was a work in progress. I saw this earth energy in my mind as being red and I saw this energy flow up through my body and out the top of my head. It connected with a higher energy above me, an energy I saw as white. This white energy was very powerful and as I breathed out I saw it filling every space inside me on its way down through my body. I felt it making its way downward, relaxing all my muscles as it filled every cell of me.

I was determined to replace the darkness inside me with light. I was determined to find every inch of it and turn it into something good. I knew this would take a long time but I was only thirty and had plenty of time at my disposal. I knew I would help myself in my mission if I could move forward with my life and function as a rational-thinking person; if I allowed myself to have a little faith and let love back into my life. The fear had taken up all the room inside me and I hadn't allowed myself to love for a long time.

Chapter Twenty-One

The first time it happened, it took me completely by surprise. My friend had a baby boy and asked me to be his godmother. I was deeply moved and wondered if she was entirely sure she wanted me as an important role model considering I was still a bit of a basket case. This all became irrelevant the first time I met him, my little godson. I instantly fell completely in love with him and had trouble recognising that warm fuzzy feeling inside my chest as love. A few tears escaped me at the miracle that just occurred, and I was so moved that I wrote a poem for him for his christening. I cherished and loved him with every part of me. I was astounded at how feeling this love for him lifted my spirits and gave me more energy.

I'd been going out more with the girls and becoming more confident being in public places packed with people. My oldest brother, Anthony, and his wife had been going out with me a lot since The Terrible Tuesday and I felt safe in their company, but I was sure they were relieved when I could go on my own. I'd even started going to the bar and the toilet by myself which was a miraculous achievement. I'd lost weight because of all the swimming, walking and the under-eating. I was ridiculously happy when at the pool my super-hot sister-in-law told me she'd never seen anyone so toned.

I was delighted that I cared at all about such a compliment for this too was an achievement. I was feeling more confident and began wearing nice clothes and a bit of make-up again. I was enjoying the summer off after completing my degree before I started my employment in September. I was still broke and in therapy but with renewed vigour that anything was possible. And then, out of nowhere, the universe knocked me on my arse again. It'll surprise you when I say I truly didn't see it coming. I'm not sure if the timing was right but I had no control over it anyway and it made absolutely no difference. Looking back now, it may have been inevitable yet such a shock to me at the same time. He, my soulmate, found me exactly when I needed to be found.

———∿∾∾∾∿∿∿———

It was incredible because he had been there the whole time – in one way or another I'd actually known him most of my life. We first met when I was about ten years old and my mum childminded his sisters. We didn't run in the same circle as teenagers but I always felt a connection to him that I couldn't explain. We saw each other occasionally and always ended up back at his mum's drinking tea and talking at the kitchen table until the early hours of the morning. Our relationship had an innocence to it that I couldn't understand, and although he always said he would phone me he never did. I never understood that either, but I didn't push it and put him firmly out of my mind when I moved to Leicester to begin my nursing career. We met in town when I came home and we arranged to go for a coffee. He collected me from my parents' and we went to a pub. I gave him an outline of The Terrible Tuesday and we both cried at the table.

He told me the story of his love life, caught between two women and in a terrible mess. We became firm friends. I was comfortable with him, relaxed in his company and tried to give him advice on his messy relationships, not that I was in a position to do so, but we had a right laugh and soon began meeting up frequently. Everyone assumed we were more than friends but we genuinely weren't, and I couldn't see how he would find me even remotely attractive in my current state of vacantness and dishevelment. I didn't consider him a potential boyfriend and certainly wasn't looking for a relationship.

When we became more than just friends I talked about it with Judy. It was terrifying contemplating another relationship I was sure would end in failure what with my therapy, shamanic work, the constant craziness and the terrible financial situation I was in, but despite all that we began the mad dance of falling in love. I tried to control every aspect of it and to hold onto everything solid to stop it from happening, much to everyone else's amusement.

I devised a point and reward system: if we did something nice for each other, we were awarded a certain number of points. It sounds silly but it was all diversionary tactics to keep it light and fun. More importantly, it was to keep my thoughts away from what would happen when he discovered the darkness inside me. I had become very good at not looking at him when we were talking. If he didn't look straight into my eyes very often, he wouldn't see what a train wreck I was on the inside. I was sure if he discovered what I was truly like, how I saw and thought about things, he would know for sure I was totally crazy and would leave me in a heartbeat.

I did everything possible to stop this from happening – I racked up so many points from being so super nice that he had to take me away somewhere for the weekend, a prospect that excited and terrified me at the same time. I wasn't good at going to new places or meeting new people but knew this was something I had to get over, and this was the perfect opportunity. So I packed my weekend case, determined I was going to have a good time, and wondered if I would need my passport. I didn't know where we were going, so decided to bring it just in case. Nothing surprised me more than when we drove to the arsehole of Donegal and down onto a back road. The road led to sand dunes and onto a beach where the P man announced with much enthusiasm that we were camping for the weekend.

Camping, as in open to the elements and wide-open spaces, did the exact same thing to my insides as being locked in a small room would have – my stomach nearly fell out my arse! I couldn't understand why he'd brought me camping, and I was seriously panicking at having to be in a tent where I could easily be attacked by some maniac with no means of escape, never mind all the bugs that made my skin crawl which would be residing with us inside the bloody tent! I couldn't possibly tell him any of this, but my face must have given me away. He looked at me, smiled warmly and said, 'Don't panic! You'll be perfectly safe here with me.' It was the first time I had no other option but to trust him when he told me it would be all right, and when he said he would keep me safe, he meant it.

So we got down to work and set up our little camp right there on the beach. I was surprised to discover it was actually quite cosy sitting in our chairs by the fire, but the P man was distraught after realising he had forgotten the pots for the stove and we couldn't make tea. My trusty old caffeine addiction meant I had brought some diet Coke, so I improvised by pouring out the Coke, filling the cans with water and putting them on the stove instead. We drank Coke-tasting tea and smoked around the fire. I couldn't help but be slightly smug about my new invention turning to him and saying, 'You see, Patrick. I'm a survivor. You could take me anywhere and I'd survive. Tea from Coke cans is a fucking genius idea, don't you think?' I was so unbelievably proud of myself that it was quite relaxing sitting there listening to the sea. I went happily to the tent and slept soundly without a nightmare or a bug in sight to disturb me. Waking early next morning, I took myself for a walk over the dunes and onto the beach. As I walked along I thought, shit, who could have imagined I could ever go camping again? That I could have relaxed enough to sleep a whole night through? I was in serious trouble – I thought I might have fallen in love with him, and I might as well just dive in instead of dipping my toes in the water. I might as well just go for it and not hold back. If it didn't work out, well, I would deal with that if the time came.'

We got serious pretty quickly after that, and I was amazed by how right it felt despite feeling so risky at the same time. We had a lot in common, wanted the same things from life and both had dogs who fell in love with each other the first time they met. That scared us both but it made our lives a lot easier that they could spend time together without killing each other. I still didn't understand how he could fall in love with me surrounded by all the craziness but he told me confidently that he thought of it as moments of crazy rather than constant crazy, which could only be a good thing. I felt so safe and relaxed with him for when he looked at me he didn't just see The Terrible Tuesday and it didn't define who I was for him. So much so that sometimes, on the good days, he even forgot about it. He saw past it and genuinely believed I would make a full recovery. He started staying over at weekends but not during the week because I felt it important to continue on my journey of being comfortable in the house by myself. However, it wasn't long before I'd extended the stay to include Monday and Thursday nights too. It was so nice to know he would be staying over with me and I looked forward to getting into bed beside him at night. It was a complete miracle. I always slept better when he was with me. He was so strong and full of light he helped me keep the darkness at bay without even knowing he was doing it.

I finished my degree and started my job. Life became busier and I was more settled into a routine of working during the week and relaxing at the weekends. I continued my sessions with Judy although they had been reduced to once a week. This reduction was a major achievement to me – there was a time I couldn't have contemplated managing a whole seven days without talking to her or discussing some aspect of my day which had driven me back into the darkness at full speed. If I found myself in the darkness, I was getting better at getting myself out of it again. I was still broken and a bit of a wreck, but I knew that on the outside at least things were looking up for me.

I was at work when my dad phoned to say there was a letter for me with an English postmark. I went to my parents' at lunchtime to see what it was – a cheque from the compensation agency in London. Whoever decides the figure you're awarded for rape – and for actual rape it's a standardised figure – must be of the same ilk as the person who made up the sentencing laws in this country. It's a ridiculously low figure. They take your job and whatnot into account, amongst other factors, before deciding how much to give you, so in my case this helped a great deal. But instead of being relieved and happy that the money had finally arrived, I was devastated. I felt they had paid me for services rendered, so to speak. I felt cheap, nasty, angry and so very upset. I had to take the afternoon off work because I couldn't stop crying, and I realised that no amount of money would have made me feel differently and no amount of money could ever have compensated me for that day.

Still, when I finally calmed down I realised how much of a relief it was to be able to pay off my debts and give everyone back the money I'd borrowed off them to keep me going along with the money they had paid out coming to the trial. It had cost everyone so much, it shouldn't have had to cost them financially as well. It was such a comfort not to be in the red any more and to pay Judy what I owed for my therapy as well. The centre didn't refuse therapy to anyone and you didn't have to pay if you couldn't afford it. That was a luxury I had benefited from for nearly three years and it was important I paid now that I could in the hope that someone else might get three years of therapy they couldn't afford but desperately needed.

I imagined I might drink the rest of the money, go on holiday or whatever – I had plenty of options at my disposal. Alas, it wasn't to be as the universe had yet another surprise in store for me – I was pregnant.

Patrick was totally and utterly delighted. I, on the other hand, was totally and utterly gobsmacked. I had this idea in my head that I couldn't have kids, or perhaps more accurately would never have kids. Honestly, I wasn't entirely sure if I wanted kids at all. Most of my working life had been spent looking after children who were very sick and didn't recover. It was so incredibly difficult to watch their parents loving them so much yet having to let them go, and I wasn't sure I could handle that sort of thing myself. Some days I couldn't even handle the inside of my own head never mind handle a baby too. I was terrified.

Around that time I took a journey with Judy. I couldn't remember the intention but when I met Cat we took the road up to the house and I was instructed to go up the stairs. I climbed until I came to a door that was locked. I knew where the key was and when I opened the door a baby was on the floor. I was incensed that someone had left a baby there all by himself and asked him how he got there and who he belonged to. Of course he couldn't answer me, but I picked him up and took him with me not wanting to leave him there on his own. When Judy and I discussed it I told her it wasn't my baby in the house and how strange it was I imagined a baby that wasn't even mine. She laughed at my conviction but it never clicked for one second it could mean I would have a baby in the not too distant future.

Five pregnancy tests later the penny finally dropped about the journey and I realised I was going to have a baby. I also knew from my journey that he was going to be a boy. Then I thought about the whole process itself – the pregnancy. How people were going to be looking at me, touching me and examining me. I thought how I was going to give birth to him and how there would undoubtedly be strange doctors, who would probably be men, looking at me and touching me without my clothes on. How the fuck was I going to do it?

It took no time at all before, in the blink of an eye, I'd done it. I'd moved The Terrible Tuesday to one side and it no longer held centre stage in my life. It no longer consumed me or my every waking moment. It no longer had the power to terrify me on the spot and stop me in my tracks. I had replaced the fear for The Terrible Tuesday with a new fear: having a baby.

Chapter Twenty-Two

I had a lot of pain in my back and down my sides, so I went to my GP. He sent me for a scan and I was told there was nothing in my womb – no sack and certainly nothing with a heartbeat. The GP explained it was probably an ectopic pregnancy and to take two weeks off work. He assured me that any subsequent pregnancy tests would eventually test negative and said that when I got severe pain to ring him as that was my body's way of telling me it was time to get the pregnancy removed. I did a pregnancy test every day for two weeks checking myself continuously for bleeding and waiting anxiously for abdominal pain.

It was only when he told me I was going to lose it that I realised how very much I wanted the baby in the first place. I prayed to God and every angel and saint in the stars to please let me keep him. I went to see an angel therapist who was also a natural healer and asked her to do some energy work around my belly. There were four magpies in her garden and if you believe in magpie folklore seeing this many in one place is a sign you'll have a baby boy. Before I even told her my name she congratulated me on my pregnancy. I explained the situation and she said I had been misinformed, that angel Gabriel brings the gift of new life and she still saw him with me in six months. She told me he was a boy and that we had had this relationship before – I had been his mummy in a previous life. She told me he would be my greatest joy and I left feeling more confident he would be all right.

After two weeks of waiting and daily pregnancy tests – all of which were positive, I went for another scan and there it was: the tiny little sack and the little beating heart. I cried so hard with relief that he was okay and in the right place that the radiographer must have thought I was completely mad. I tried really hard not to smoke, to eat healthy food and not to think too much about The Terrible Tuesday in case I unintentionally transmitted it to the baby, which was really difficult at times, but it was the tiredness at the start that was excruciating, never mind the constant puking that should not be called morning sickness when it lasts all day, and the pain in my chest – I thought someone had replaced my boobs with two giant rocks when I wasn't looking.

I was nauseous all day and extremely grumpy in the evening. I couldn't remember anyone ever telling me how miserable it was to be pregnant! I was patiently waiting to feel the joy of pregnancy but could never relax enough to allow myself to enjoy it. Patrick had taken over the nesting phase by redecorating the house and sorting out the nursery, and I could only look on in horror at what was to come and just how much he relished this turn of events in our relationship. I enjoyed pregnancy a lot more once I could feel him move inside me – his constant kicking and the terrible heartburn assured me he was very much alive, well and getting ready to make an appearance.

I was astounded at people's curiosity with my belly and their constant need to touch it as if it wasn't a part of me; as if they didn't have to ask for my permission before they ran their hands all over my stomach and invaded my personal space. I stayed in quite a bit to avoid this scenario, entirely focused on worrying about the impending birth and how I would get through it without having a complete breakdown.

―――――✦✦✦―――――

I went privately to a female gynaecologist, and after worrying about it for nine straight months, I had a caesarean section when five days overdue. After all my worrying I didn't encounter a single strange man or give birth myself. They just airlifted him out of my stomach and held him up for me to see. My first thought was oh my God, it's a real live baby! as though I was expecting a doll. I was surprised by the pain in my chest when he cried, and I wanted to jump off the theatre trolley, rip him out of their arms and bury him inside me again so I could protect him from ever being hurt, afraid or alone. I didn't know if it was because of The Terrible Tuesday that my overwhelming emotion when my baby cried was fear and not love, but I was terrified they would hurt him and

I couldn't stop them. I would have killed to protect him and it scared the crap out of me.

I didn't get a rush of overwhelming love that some women describe when they first see their baby, but love came hand in hand with the fear I felt; I realised I was so scared because I loved him so much. I couldn't understand where he came from, this little creature who had achieved so much in his short time here, having graciously relegated The Terrible Tuesday to one side of me. I had these wonderful thoughts about the role he played in my recovery, and also how I'd seen him somewhere before – maybe we had been here before this lifetime in a similar role to we were now. I thought I'd been his mummy forever he was so familiar to me.

Then came the practical stuff: the crying, feeding, pooing and no sleeping was pretty hard to handle on a continual basis. The feeling of not recognising yourself in the mirror and looking like a fat, wobbly monster with extremely large boobs and a saggy belly was just so utterly depressing. I had re-employed my habit of not looking in the mirror and it worked out rather nicely. I didn't even care what I looked like any more. There was also the irritation of his daddy snoring beside me in a blissful state of contented ignorance at the thought of his son and the whole four hours of the day he actually spent with him. What might have been worse was the aggravating realisation that life hadn't changed much for Daddy and he still had to get a good night's sleep to head to work in the morning. I, however, could be up most of the night and the day too because I wasn't leaving the house to go out to work. No, the other twenty hours of the day when his daddy was either sleeping or working was up to me; the responsibility of him lay heavily within me. What if something happened to him? What if he stopped breathing in the night and I didn't hear him? What if someone took him away? What if something *bad* happened to him? And I couldn't bear to think of what bad might actually entail, so I also had a television and newspaper ban to stop me from freaking out altogether.

I continually worried about what would happen if I couldn't protect him from whatever was coming for him. What then? I was on high alert at all times and I'd already timed my breathing with his – one short delay and I was out of bed leaning over the crib to make sure he was still with me. I hardly let him out of my sight during the day in case something happened to him while I wasn't watching.

I wasn't sure if I was being a psycho or if these were normal thoughts to have with a first baby. Everyone assumed I was perfectly capable of caring for him because I was a nurse and knew more than most about babies, but they didn't realise it was so different having a baby of my own. I was totally unprepared for how much it changed me. As well as being terrified of him and for him, I was so proud of him and I couldn't wait for him to meet Judy as if he was proof of my achievement.

I couldn't wait to tell her The Terrible Tuesday had lost its prime slot in my head and now came a boring old second to my son. I couldn't wait to tell her it would never be first place inside my head again because then my son might think he wasn't good enough to hold my centre stage. I wouldn't allow him to think that. I couldn't wait to see her and tell her my wonderful thoughts about my little son. We mutually decided I was going to stop seeing her, stop having therapy sessions and see what happened when I went it alone. I was going to focus on my new role as a mother and I was going to cope with it on my own. Well, that was the plan, but I was unsure as to how it would all pan out in reality. I was excited she thought I was ready to stop therapy and nervous because I still thought I wasn't quite ready to give her up. In fact, I wasn't ready at all. I wasn't sure if I would fall apart at the seams or if I would know what to do without her, but I knew I had to try and I would give it my best shot. When I took him to meet her we decided that would be our last meeting.

———⋙⋘———

My last appointment was on the third anniversary of The Terrible Tuesday. It was fitting to both of us that our last meeting was on that day, and it was the first anniversary that didn't hold the same meaning for me. I still couldn't sleep and still had terrible nightmares but most of my waking moments were consumed by my new baby and meeting his needs before my own. I spent the whole hour desperately trying not to cry because I wanted to show her I was a strong, independent woman who was no longer restricted in daily life by the events of The Terrible Tuesday. I wanted to show her she had achieved her objective and could congratulate herself on a job well done. Judy held my baby for our entire session and I was delighted she was so taken with him. She seemed to genuinely appreciate the little miracle she held in her arms. We talked of her own little ones and of being a mother. The insight into how she raised her children was fascinating and through our conversation I found that it was perfectly normal to have all those thoughts as a first-time mother. I was dismayed at the thought of not seeing her again and only just stopped myself from saying, 'Can we not just be friends?' and asking to meet for coffee almost as though she was an ex-boyfriend I was trying to get back with, and although I thought we had a close relationship I was still aware she was a professional and that this was her job, what she did for a living and not who she was. It seemed so much more to her than just a job, so I wondered if the professional boundaries were a little looser. Could I not just ask her for coffee? I thought of the parents of the children I worked with who asked me to stay in touch and to meet up after they lost their children. No matter how much I liked them, really wanted to stay friendly and meet up, I knew it wouldn't be very professional. I also couldn't do that for every one of them because I simply wouldn't have had enough time. I tried to say no but there were occasions when I broke my own rule: when I was confident parents needed to stay in touch with me, that I was a link to their child they couldn't let go of, but I knew these parents would let go of me in time. Then there were still parents I kept in touch with, even now. Those parents *I* couldn't let go of for whatever reason. Sometimes you make a connection with people and it lasts a lifetime no matter how it began. So I thought deeply about asking Judy for a coffee and decided I didn't want it to be a we-are-not-sure-if-I-still-need-therapy coffee, that it should be a I-let-go-of-her-in-time coffee. I knew then that I wouldn't mention coffee or meeting up as friends.

When it was time for us to leave – the P man came to collect us because I couldn't drive after my C-section – Judy and I were both crying. I felt like I was saying goodbye to my second mother, and I couldn't thank her like I wanted to before I started crying. I did the best I could and continued crying long after we'd arrived home. I told myself it was my hormones because I didn't have time to think properly about why I was crying this long and hard. I was crying because I no longer needed therapy and I no longer needed Judy. I was crying with relief it was over and with sadness because I had left her. I was crying that I'd ever had to go to her in the first place. I was crying for the person I was when I first met her and because I was grateful for the person I'd become. I knew it was partly because of her that I was the new me, and

I should have told her that but I couldn't because the crying wouldn't stop long enough to get the words out. I couldn't believe my last appointment was over and I felt so sad I wouldn't be seeing her again.

I tried my best to do without her. I stopped my shamanic work and my meditation and promptly went back to ignoring my intuitive side. In general I ignored myself so I could focus everything I had on the baby. I was walking a tightrope enjoying the light and love in my life with Patrick and our son while balancing the darkness within me and not letting fear overwhelm me. I was exhausted from trying to keep steady all the time.

———✺✺✺———

Some days the darkness won and I couldn't let the baby out of my sight much less out for a walk with his granny, and Patrick would give me the you-are-being-fucking-ridiculous look, but it couldn't be helped and I wouldn't change my mind. I couldn't explain it to him in a way he would understand either — the knot in my stomach and the overwhelming fear something would happen to my baby when I wasn't there. Other days I would be happy to leave him for a little while, and Patrick would be delighted to come home and find I had actually dressed and left the house and could talk about something other than every minute spent amusing our son. I tried my hardest to entertain him when his eyes were open to stimulate and speed his brain development so he would grow faster and do things for himself quicker. Even the baby started to look at me weirdly when I did my baby-talk voice; he much preferred his daddy's relaxed company to my watchful, anxious eyes upon him. He smiled and talked much more to his daddy in the evenings than he did to me the entire day. I saw this as proof of my high anxiety levels and made a huge effort to just relax and let him do his own thing.

I loved being on maternity leave but I had a permanent contract with the trust. My sister-in-law was a childminder and she agreed to mind my son, which allayed my fears about leaving him. It was comforting that I knew her really well, that she genuinely loved him and that I knew she would never harm him. I couldn't have returned to work if I had had to leave him with a random childminder having decided you could never really know if a person had darkness in them unless you spent quality time with them.

Chapter Twenty-Three

Despite this, I underestimated how difficult it was to leave him every day and I cried the entire way to work. A full forty minutes of weeping only to arrive laden with guilt at having left him with someone else coupled with the fear something would happen to him when I wasn't there. I was miserable at work and then I was miserable at home because of being at work in the first place. I was missing out on all the fun at home and watching him grow and develop. I had to know how many dirty bums he'd had, every morsel he ate, exactly what he played with and how long he slept for. I drove my sister-in-law mad with continual phone calls and text messages throughout the day.

He didn't indulge my overprotective streak for very long and made it clear from the start he was an independent little soul. At sixteen weeks he held his own bottle and wouldn't let me hold it for him again after that. He slept with his hands behind his head without a care in the world and that became my favourite part of the day – feeding him lunch and then watching him sleep for an hour or so. He never crawled but walked at ten months. He had reflux and cows' milk protein allergy, sitting up in his cot every night to vomit only to lie back down and go straight back to sleep. He was frequently sick – not significantly but he had continual infections, and although the paediatrician discovered his immune system was below par, we were reassured he would grow out of it as he got bigger.

The reflux, the vomiting and the sickness took more out of me than him and he thrived despite it. At fifteen months he said he wanted to do a pee-pee and that was the end of nappies. He was a strong, placid, sturdy wee boy – a joy to be around. When he was about eighteen months old I decided that although I didn't particularly want to have another baby I also didn't want him to be an only child, so I talked to the P man about having another baby. He didn't want him to be an only child either and we wanted them be close enough in age to enjoy each other. We decided to go for it and planned another addition to the family.

———— ~~~~~~~~~~~~~~ ————

We tried to get out and about and make the most of our weekends, so when Patrick suggested we take the dogs to the Gortin Lakes one Saturday morning I thought nothing of it – that was until he suggested we all go in his pick-up. I thought he was acting weird, so I insisted on taking my own car. We got to our usual picnic bench and sat down to watch the dogs swim. All of a sudden he was on one knee in front of me, telling me just how much he loved me, especially since we'd had the baby. He was telling me just how happy he was and I was wondering why he was sweating when daylight dawned. He was proposing! I felt sick and said, 'Please get up from there. Seriously, Patrick, you're scaring me!' He laughed and took the ring out of his pocket. 'Will you marry me?' he asked. I was so shocked I didn't say anything at all. I thought he was joking – he couldn't seriously want to marry me with all my craziness. Enough time passed for him to utter, 'Are you going to say something?'

I quickly snapped out of it and said, 'Yes. Yes, of course I'll marry you, but will you please get up!' He went behind the trees and brought out a picnic, blankets and champagne. We had a picnic in the sun but couldn't open the champagne because I'd stubbornly insisted on bringing my own car. I wanted to go home and share the news with my parents and was ecstatic when Patrick told me they already knew and he had asked my dad's permission. He laughed relaying the story of Daddy telling him he was a bit late in asking seeing as he had already got me 'up the duff'. I knew my daddy would have been chuffed at being asked anyway. We went out to celebrate, the baby having a sleepover at his nanny's so we could have a lie-in. The entire evening I thought he must be mad, that there was something wrong with his head to have chosen me.

I called in to see Judy and told her my news. It was so good to see her and show her how big the baby was. She was genuinely so very happy for me that it was almost like meeting up with an old friend. It was obvious that love and light had tipped the scales in my favour and I was winning the battle with the darkness. It was also obvious that The Terrible Tuesday didn't hold centre stage in my life, although I did wonder how long this reprieve would last – no nightmares, flashbacks, panic attacks and not thinking about it for days on end. I cherished it and hoped it would last forever. We stayed in celebration mode for a few months and then tried for another baby. I got pregnant straightaway and enjoyed my pregnancy much more second time round. It helped that my C-section was planned in advance.

We didn't find out the gender of the baby, although I knew it was a girl. I couldn't decide whether I was delighted or terrified about having another baby or whether the problem was that she was a girl. I was unsure if I could possibly love her as much as I loved my son and wondered if there would be room inside me for both of them. Luckily I didn't have too much time to dwell on it between working full-time, having a toddler and being pregnant. I decided not to think about it until she made an appearance.

———⁓ᴡᴏᴏᴏᴇᴛᴏᴏᴛᴏᴏᴏᴡᴡ———

My planned caesarean felt much more relaxed. That was until I got the shock of my life when they held her up for me to see and I registered a head full of mental red hair – never mind her screaming having been so rudely plucked from my belly. My stomach was in knots, I couldn't breathe properly and was about to be sick, so they gave her to her daddy and he whisked her out of theatre while they stitched me up and gave me sickness meds. I heard her crying the whole time and, again, I wanted to jump off the trolley to go and get her. The anxiety in my stomach never went away despite the medication but I thought it was probably due to being in hospital and not getting any sleep. Things would be fine when we got home, and, I suppose looking back, the first few weeks were okay. Her brother was really keen on her and all the extra attention he was getting. All in all, she was quite settled. I was breastfeeding and until she was three weeks old, her routine was to simply feed and sleep. But suddenly I didn't have enough milk for her, and I had a nasty infection in my stomach and had to take strong painkillers and antibiotics which were making her sick. I stopped the feeding and switched her to formula milk but she had a complete mental and physical meltdown: vomiting all the time, never pooing and developing dreadful eczema.

Her skin was not only red and blotchy but was literally falling off, especially on her face. And she *never* stopped crying. No matter what I did, what I fed her or how long I rocked her she cried non-stop. The fear moved back into my belly and I was so distracted by her and the noise of her that it took over my body until I ended up terrified of her and for her. We knew she was allergic to the milk and had reflux, so we changed her formula and gave her medication, but it made no difference to the vomiting or her crying. She never slept for more than an hour or two at a time and vomited so much I spent all my time feeding and then re-feeding her.

We went for the first of many trips to hospital to try to alleviate her pain and improve her insides. As time went on I became increasingly angry with every person who looked at her, touched her and examined her. My insides were out of control. I couldn't eat and the pooing was back with a vengeance. I'd gone way past being mildly irritated all the time to wanting to kill someone nearly all of the time. I could hardly breathe I was so fearful for her all the time. I couldn't do it any more, so I decided enough was enough and I stopped them examining her unless it was absolutely necessary and refused to let them take her bloods more than once. I insisted on doing all her nursing care myself and was angry, difficult and upset. I just wanted to lift her and run where no one would find us.

It didn't help when my two-year-old son told me his sister wanted to go home. I said, 'She is home, honey.' To which he replied, 'No, Mummy, I mean home in the sky,' and pointed to the ceiling. I thought that meant she was going to die; that maybe looking after all those children who had died had led me to this road where my own child would die too. The universe must have really hated me to knock me on my ass again so soon.

———∽∿◦◦∾◦◦∾∿◦◦∿———

I couldn't believe this was happening, that I had to watch her in pain all the time and let them touch her tiny body over and over again *without her permission* knowing that that was the one thing I had most trouble doing, knowing that it would drive me over the edge in my own head and body. I was losing my mind again. I thought about The Terrible Tuesday all the time and my senses were on high alert and in constant protection mode. I felt like a tiger ready and waiting to pounce and attack. Patrick and I were continually fighting over anything and everything but mainly about how much sleep he got and how much sleep I didn't get – a very sensitive subject. I was drowning under the weight of everything.

Between the continual cleaning of puke and the never-ending crying, I had to deal with a toddler, Patrick, The Terrible Tuesday, the house and keep myself together with no sleep. I just couldn't manage it all at the one time. It was too much for me and I knew it. I felt the presence of other people and saw things in my bedroom at night. I could hear them too and it was then that I really thought I'd lost the plot

I was persuaded to visit my GP and he diagnosed postnatal depression. He gave me antidepressants and told me to come back in a month. I really must have been in a bad way as I didn't even have antidepressants after The Terrible Tuesday and that was rock bottom for me. At least I seriously hoped it was. I looked at the tablets and noticed a warning on the box that they may cause drowsiness. I put them back in their box. I couldn't afford to be drowsy in case she died in her sleep and I wouldn't let her do that to me.

The time had come and, although I didn't want to, I rang Judy to make an appointment before something awful happened. I needed to see her before I completely cracked up. I was worried she would think she had failed me and I was a basket case again, yet I was surprised it took two and a half years before I had to make an appointment – surprised I kept the darkness out of me for so long. I rang and to my utter disappointment she was in bloody Australia. I had to hold it together until she came back and I could see her again.

In that first appointment I don't think she said anything at all, just listened while I cried, raged and told her all about my daughter and what she had done to my insides. She asked me if I loved her and I paused as if to think about it. I hadn't given any thought as to whether I loved her or not because I was so consumed with fear. I cried all the harder then because of course I loved her – it was because I loved her that she scared me so much. I cried because I was heartbroken that her first memory of me was that I let them touch her without her permission and because of that I felt I had failed her.

I told Judy I felt like I had backtracked on all the progress I had made over The Terrible Tuesday, and how once again I was consumed by the fear and the terror of it all. All I could concentrate on was the awfulness and panic over something potentially happening to my daughter. Not only that, I was consumed with thoughts of my own mother and how she must have felt for me. I only now totally understood her complete devastation and anger with me when I lived in her house during some of my darkest days. I wished I could turn back time and eat everything she asked me to eat. I wished I hadn't fought with her so much. I was amazed at her stamina in sticking with me for the long haul and being such an important part of my recovery.

I felt so guilty because I told my mother I didn't think I could cope with my daughter for much longer. She told me having such thoughts was fine and she would help me with her. She sat with me many a night in my living room helping me clean puke and nursed my daughter for hours on end unfazed by the continual crying when I was at absolute breaking point. There was nothing my mother wouldn't do for me and I realised that was exactly the same for me and my little wailing redhead. I just felt so useless not being able to help her or soothe her or console her. I was at a loss as to what to do for her and myself – for my insides and my head.

Chapter Twenty-Four

I told Judy Patrick and I were worlds apart and I couldn't explain to him how I felt about our daughter or how my insides had turned upside down again. I told him I felt anxiousness in my stomach all the time and that my nerves were seriously fried with lack of sleep and continual sickness but I knew he didn't understand why I was so angry all the time, especially with him. He just didn't know how I felt. He got away so lightly, so confident that she would be fine in the long run. He didn't see the world as I did and hadn't experienced the darkness; I seriously envied him that luxury so much so there were times I wanted to punch him in the face. I told Judy I was seriously worried we wouldn't make it and I would end up a single mother with two children I couldn't cope with.

I apologised most sincerely at having to come back to therapy but she said it wasn't a problem and that I was in a bit of a pickle. I was relieved my phone call was warranted but I was also gutted I needed to see her again. I just had to suck it up and get on with it. I just had to revisit my old nightmare and nemesis, The Terrible Tuesday. I would just have to get to the bottom of it this time, to the very root of it, and pull it up from the ground completely if I was ever to be free of it and if my daughter was ever to have some semblance of a normal life without mine coming tumbling down around her.

How was I going to find the time to do that in between looking after my children, not having a nervous breakdown and salvaging my relationship. There wouldn't be enough hours in the day to fit it all in until I remembered I was up most of the night as well. So at night when I was sitting up with my daughter, I looked within myself at the darkness messing up my insides and at the things in my head. I made a plan of how to improve things and how to let them go. *Really* let them go this time. The first thing I did was to properly accept, in every part of my being, that The Terrible Tuesday had truly happened to me. I had never truly owned it or embraced it as being part of who I was and I still felt dodgy accepting it. If I truly accepted it had happened, would I be saying that because it happened it was allowed to happen – that it was okay almost? I never wanted to be okay with it happening.

I agreed to go back to my writing – I had started writing a journal after The Terrible Tuesday but had stopped after the trial and never finished it. It hung over me like a dark cloud because it was incomplete on paper and therefore incomplete in my head. I agreed I would go back to it and finish the story. I agreed I would revisit it once more in my head and my heart in an effort to finish it and be rid of it. I told Judy about my nightly visitations making a reappearance and that I could hear them. She said I obviously wasn't listening to them, that I had nothing to be afraid of because they were only trying to help me through my current crisis. I decided to let them in.

I was going to have to accept that weird part of myself, the spiritual side, and embrace it as part of who I was, who I always was even before The Terrible Tuesday. Ignoring it would only get me in more trouble with the universe. I learned how to protect myself against unwelcome visitors and any dark energies coming my way. I learned to think of these things as perfectly reasonable to have in my head and I learned not be freaked out by them.

Judy and I decided to take up our shamanic work again as that too felt incomplete. I felt guilty having abandoned Cat for so long and I hoped she would still be my friend when I got there, but almost as soon as I arrived I had a new guide who told me it was all about balance and I was seriously unbalanced. He reminded me to bring the energy from the earth right up through my body and back down again filled with light and to fill my insides with it and replace all the darkness inside and around me. He showed me how to meditate to reach the quiet place in me and to just let that quietness breathe for a moment in between all the madness that filled my day. I needed to be more centred, more grounded and more balanced if I was to keep the darkness at bay; meditation and energy work would help me do that.

Judy told me to focus on the love I had for my daughter and that became my little mantra: think about the love, think about the love, think about the love. Every time she puked, choked, cried and drove me crazy I reminded myself to think about the love I had for her in my heart and not to focus on my exhaustion and tension. I was instantly more relaxed with her and I knew she could tell because she smiled at me more and cried at me less. At nine months old she began sleeping for four consecutive hours – a miracle. I took her to reiki and craniosacral therapy and she seemed more relaxed and happier in herself. I continually linked my heart with hers when I was doing energy work with her. Because of this I felt more connected to her, more than I ever felt before, and although she wasn't getting much better, I was getting much better at coping with her. I was getting stronger, more centred and much more balanced and I hadn't taken any antidepressants.

In the midst of one of our hospital stays with our daughter and my wobbly progress with the darkness my father had a heart attack. I immediately didn't care about his heart attack or how bad it was as long as he didn't die. I just couldn't cope with my father dying on top of everything else. My faith, which had been *seriously* lacking of late, came jumping into action and I thought my father would be okay, my father would sail through his heart surgery and be here for another while because I was nowhere near ready to let him go. That was the only thought I entertained in my head and I realised I had turned a bit of a corner in not thinking dark thoughts or giving in to the fear that my father would die. I gave them no power and they didn't exist for me. I got determination from somewhere and I was unfazed when our daughter had to go into hospital again. I was getting such relief talking to Judy about her every week and I could almost put it into perspective, how she made me feel on the inside, and acknowledge how difficult it was to look after her but also how it wouldn't last forever.

She would, of course, grow out of her reflux within the next couple of years and shouldn't have any long-lasting ill effects from it. She probably wouldn't remember she had ever had it and would laugh at me when I told her what she was like as a baby. I managed to get more time off work so I could stay at home with her, which meant our son didn't have to go to the childminder any more. I was delighted and finally felt guilt-free because

I was looking after him myself ... although some days, between the two of them and the continual crying, I found myself wishing I was at work.

———∿∽◦◦◦◦∽∿———

I continued journeying and started to read about the chakra system, energy work and about shamanism and how to use it in everyday life. I put it into practice in my home life, with my children and in my relationship. Things improved at home and it became more like family life and less like a war zone. I went on a residential weekend called The Shaman's Journey and was amazed to discover just how far I'd come on my journey through the darkness which had been long and unyielding but which I hoped was almost at the end. It was seven years since The Terrible Tuesday and I had come so far. I was amazed at the progress I'd made and what I'd achieved so far in my recovery.

I told Patrick all about my therapy this time and tried to explain how I was feeling. We talked more and fought less as time went on. Our daughter had her first birthday and we were both so relieved to have survived the nightmare that was her first year and knew that things could only get better in her second year. As she got bigger and stronger her health would only improve and we were both convinced she would eventually sleep through the night. My brother and his wife across the lane were very good with her and not at all phased by the puking or the crying. They agreed to look after her so we could have a few nights out and a few nights away. That did the trick in restoring the balance between us.

I had let go of the anxiety in my stomach and I hadn't had any dark thoughts overwhelming my insides for a while. I was feeling much better and much brighter, so maybe a combination of things had worked to make me more balanced – therapy, shamanic work, meditation and spending time with Patrick alone lifted my energy levels and my general mood despite continuing not to get much sleep. There were more days when I won the battle but still plenty when I simply didn't, when I was irrational, angry and panicky over the smallest things. However, there were days when I was none of those things and there were *even* days when I didn't think about The Terrible Tuesday at all.

———∿∽◦◦◦◦∽∿———

I read somewhere that every cell in the human body regenerated on a seven-year cycle, and I was delighted when it was the seventh anniversary of The Terrible Tuesday. That cycle was coming to an end for me and I was determined to pull it up from the very ground before then. I was determined I would be balanced before this cycle was finished and I would do whatever it took to reach the very roots of it and pull them out so I would never have to do it again. If I didn't do it this time, I thought that cycle of The Terrible Tuesday would come around again and I would have to do it all over again from scratch. I didn't know if that was true, but I couldn't take the chance of it coming around again, so I had to push myself to the finish line.

On the anniversary, at around ten thirty that morning, there wasn't one cell left in my body that he had had his slimy, disgusting hands on. I was delighted that from the inside out I was brand new and untouched by him or anyone else, and I thought that that was my body's way of doing what it could to forget it. I was hoping that would put paid to the physical reminders of The Terrible Tuesday that occurred of their own free will twice a year: the anniversaries of that day and of the trial. I was thrilled with the notion that after this anniversary the next time Patrick touched me would be for the first time too.

By finishing this journal I had done what I could to put it out of my head and out of my body, and I would work continuously to keep it out of my energy zone and that of my children's. I read about past lives – that we are all spiritual beings on a physical journey, and I knew that The Terrible Tuesday was an important curve in the road for me. If I kept on walking, I would eventually come to the end of that curve and onto a new part in the road. The longer I walked, the closer I'd get to it and the closer I'd get to being free of it. Eventually, when I look back, I won't be able to see it in the distance at all. I felt like I was coming full circle and was finally reaching a stage when I would truly be able to let it go. I was in a grateful phase – like in the very beginning when I was grateful just to be alive and breathing, and the phases were overlapping before I could move forward with only gratefulness to guide me.

Chapter Twenty-Five

I went on a weekend meditation course that focused on opening my heart to heal, and through my shamanic journeying I had done that. I had replaced all the darkness inside me with light. I went on a journey, deep down to Mother Earth, and I stood under a fountain of light which flowed effortlessly through every cell in my body and around me. I was luminous, light as a feather and given a new power animal, a tiger, to take with me. I was taken to the garden of my flat in London with Cat and the tiger, and I knew exactly what day and what time it was as I made my way into the flat.

I knew exactly what I would find in the bedroom when I saw myself on the bed. I could see the dark energy filling my bedroom and I knew this was why I had to be completely filled with light – so I could stand on equal footing with it and not be afraid or consumed by it. I got frustrated with the continual messages from spirits to meditate, meditate, meditate, fill myself with light, over and over again but now I understood its purpose as I stood at the door and watched what was happening to me. Yet I didn't feel any fear.

I watched with horror as the darkness consumed her and her light dimmed. I *willed* her to hang on until they went to the bathroom. I realised with absolute clarity that it couldn't be undone, no part of it could be changed and I couldn't intervene, and it was with incredible sadness that I watched the darkness and light, that girl on the bed and that dark thing posing as a human. There was not one bit of light within that dark thing and I watched as she was lifted into the air by the dark thing and saw a light imprint of her left behind on the bed.

It was all starting to make sense, and I followed them down the hall waiting patiently in the bathroom for him to leave. I saw her look in the mirror and as I stared back at my own reflection, I heard my own voice declare, 'I know you're here. I need some help. I need to get out of this bathroom and I need you to show me the way,' and I knew that was my moment. I knew it was me who showed her the way out. I told her what to do and I moved her to the cupboard and guided her hands to the scissors. I moved her to the door and I stood with her and held her hands steady as she loosened the bolts in the lock. 'I am here,' I told her over and over again, and although I knew she couldn't hear me, I knew she could *feel* me.

The tiger moved to stand behind her and the three of us became one as he gave her the strength to open the door, and this time I heard the tiger roar at the precise moment I opened my mouth and let out a guttural scream. The sound was almost deafening as the energy carried within it as well as the strength we had together forced the lock to break off the wall and the door to finally open.

I told her there was no time and he was on his way back down Dalston High Street at this very minute and she must hurry. I went with her to the bedroom and watched her dress and I knew she would stop for the cigarettes in the kitchen. Then I moved her to the front door and I showed her the nuns' house which was surrounded by a white light. I pushed her out the door, telling her to go, shouting at her to run, and I watched until she made it safely to the white light and I could hear her knock on their door. I retraced my steps back through the flat and out to the back garden. Back through the same route I had come and back with Cat and the tiger to the tree and the tunnel and finally back to reality.

I was astounded by this journey. Astounded at the profound healing that took place within me and astounded at the significance of it as I did indeed only bring a part of myself back from London. I had finally come full circle with that awful day. I had solved the mystery in the bathroom, of whose presence I felt, along with the mystery of whom I asked for help and who showed me the way out. How ironic that it was me who helped myself that day.

I was delighted at how energised I felt after the weekend meditation course, and while I was abundantly aware it all sounded a bit strange, I'm compelled to say that it wasn't about how it sounded but about how I felt, and I felt I had finally been shown the bigger picture of that day, that I had finally reached inside myself and turned the lights back on. I was a completely different person on the inside and in how I managed my feelings. The fear, anxiety and panic had left me. I had no way of knowing if it was for good this time, but I felt that between Judy and my shamanic work I had been given the tools I needed for my personal and spiritual development. Between meditation, energy work and yoga practice I would be doing everything I could to keep the balance within myself and in my environment on an energetic level.

My daughter's health was gradually improving and both my children had reached that lovely age of being able to talk back. I found them both so challenging and entertaining in equal measure that I dreaded the thought of returning to work and leaving them with a childminder. I didn't want to return yet again to the madness of full-time work with two young children along with the guilt I would carry with me every day because it wasn't me looking after them. I wasn't sure I had it in me to leave them for such a huge part of their day when they were so young.

I asked the universe very nicely to please make it possible for me to stay at home with them until they started school and didn't need me as much. I remained hopeful this would happen. The residential weekend I went on was the first time I had ever done shamanic work for someone else and was surprised by how much I enjoyed it. I was also surprised at how I had never given any thought to journeying for someone else or doing energy work for other people. I felt as though this was an area I would like to explore in the future.

As our children neared the grand old ages of two and four, The P man and I were miraculously still on track for the whole marriage thingy – if we could ever afford it. I told him there was a time when I thought we were never going to make it and I was seriously worried about being a single mother. He laughed and told me he was never worried – not even for a minute, and he always knew we would be okay in the end. I felt dreadful for ever having doubted us and was resolute it would never happen again. We had a lovely wee family, the four of us and the dogs, and generally we were very happy.

I was glad to find I'd started to care about myself again and I was able to take off all my clothes and look in the mirror. I mean, *really* look at myself. A body after two C-sections is not a pretty sight, but I started personal training sessions and tried not to eat chocolate – a work in progress. I was relieved I was starting to look like my old self again and was losing the is-she-or-isn't-she-pregnant look. I was feeling more confident in my own skin and I enjoyed making an effort with myself. The swimming pool had closed but I started walking more with my friends and by myself.

I had been so lucky to have so many good friends help and support me over the last seven years but I had also been unlucky enough to lose touch with so many good friends too. I had lost touch with so many good people in London, that was a matter of geography on my part because we weren't in the same country to catch up with each other and I wasn't good at keeping up with phone calls and emails. I would like to visit them all again some day, to go to my old ward and properly say my goodbyes face-to-face. Rachel and I were still good friends and kept in touch with her continuing to visit me despite me not returning the favour. I remained good friends with the girls and grew closer to some more than others but that too was a matter of geography and timing. We all tried to spend time together on a regular basis and two were getting married which was exciting for all of us. I'd made some new friends along the way too and picked up my social life again. I enjoyed going out and having a glass of wine and was ecstatic when my brother Paul sent me on a trip to Madrid to visit Anne who was teaching English there. Paul flew in from Germany and the three of us had a cracker weekend.

I was continually working on all the limitations in my life because of The Terrible Tuesday and I forced myself to go to the dentist before my teeth fell out. I went once, not long after I had come home, because I had an awful pain in my jaw and couldn't eat. He pulled out my wisdom tooth, which was growing into my cheek, with something resembling a pair of pliers. It took a lot longer than it should have because I had around ten panic attacks with him being so close to me, looming over me almost, and I couldn't breathe. I couldn't let him give me any pain relief either in case it made me drowsy because I needed to be in complete control. I ended up in excruciating pain and spat blood for three days.

I couldn't shake the habit of changing my bedroom around every summer. I moved furniture, painted, decorated and bought new quilts and curtains all in an effort to feel more comfortable. It made me feel more at ease and I found it easier to sleep for a while but it wasn't long before I wanted to do it all over again. This year, however, the P man put his foot down and said I wasn't allowed to change anything, that it was fine as it was. I had to give in and just deal with it, but I managed to sneak in a new quilt cover telling him it was only twenty quid in town, and I still had to actively work on not feeling compelled to do the bedroom up.

———⟋ᴗᴏᴄᴏ⟋ᴏᴑᴑᴏ⟋ᴏᴑ⟍———

The biggest outstanding goal I had yet to achieve was the completion of this piece of writing, my journal, which turned into this manuscript. It had been the most surprising and most difficult part to see through to the end. I set myself a deadline to be finished before the seventh anniversary of The Terrible Tuesday, which is only a few weeks away, so despite all the pain it causes me I must push on and complete it. The motivation for my writing has mostly been fuelled by the anger that was inside me. I apologise most sincerely if this manuscript has an angry undertone to it, but it couldn't be helped. I had to release it and this was the perfect avenue with which to do it. I was spurred on by my outrage at the outing of a well-known television personality and his abuse and violation that spanned decades, and by my anger that made me want to punch anyone who mentioned his name. I wanted to retreat to the good old days of denial and the vacant place in my head. I wanted to go back to television and magazine censoring when I wouldn't have heard or seen anything about it as my mental state was so fragile at the thought of it.

So I pushed my way through. I felt such an overall sadness having to write that it ever happened in the first place, but I have truly accepted that it has and I can't change it. Now that I have almost come to the end of my writing, I'm thinking about what I want to do with it and I feel a change in the air and a shift of energy.

It took some time to notice that it wasn't just me, that every time I turned on the television or picked up a newspaper, some other celebrity was being arrested; that there are far more stories of people being charged with sex crimes now, and I think this could be the start of a new movement where these crimes won't be tolerated any more. I want to be part of that movement. I want to share my story with other people in the hope that they will see what a difficult road I've been on since that day and that they will see and understand what The Terrible Tuesday did to me physically and mentally.

I've been writing and rewriting this manuscript for as long as I can remember, and Judy has read every draft. We have then discussed it and how it has made me feel, and I have finally come to the stage where I'm happy with it. I'm happy with the knowledge that this is my story, every sad and painful part of it. Every word on every page is a part of it and I have realised that I've let it go with each chapter I've written.

We decided I no longer *needed* therapy when Judy told me the centre was closing because they had lost their funding and could no longer operate. The irony of this made me laugh – what other way would there be to end it other than the place closing down and Judy no longer working there?

I felt so relieved it didn't close down when I was only a year or two into my therapy because then I really would have had a complete breakdown. Were it not for my sessions with Judy, I would never have come this far in my recovery and wouldn't be so healthy in my head. I felt so fortunate for having had the opportunity to work with her. I felt so fortunate she empowered me to journey for myself and for the spiritual development it brought into my life. It's really sad that other people with problems like I had won't get the opportunity to work with her.

We both knew our last appointment was looming, and I would like Judy to stay in touch with me this time – not because I *need* her to but because I'd *like* her to, and I felt sure our paths would cross again. She had been such an important part of my recovery and I would be forever grateful to her for the person I'd become. I wasn't looking forward to saying goodbye to her because I knew it would definitely be for the last time with her as my therapist. We discussed the central-focus phrase and I could honestly say that The Terrible Tuesday didn't have central focus inside me any more. It didn't even have left or right focus most days, and I was hoping that would be the last year my body remembered it too and then it would have no focus at all. There was a sadness in saying goodbye to it, for it had become as familiar as an old friend. In saying that, there was also such an overwhelming sense of relief that I'd finished it and I couldn't wait to live life without it hanging over me. I knew it would be another work in progress to add to the list but I was determined to stay on top of this battle we were having with the darkness and I was determined to fill my world with light.

As spooky as it sounded, I'd decided to have a fire-burning ceremony in my garden once the seventh anniversary passed. The P man had built a huge sandstone firepit out the back and it was the perfect place to burn everything to do with The Terrible Tuesday and keep only this manuscript. This will be my only legacy to it. I was going to burn all the paperwork and newspaper articles I'd kept since that day. All the correspondence relating to it was going up in smoke. It would be symbolic in the letting go of it all and I was looking forward to opening the wardrobe without seeing it hidden deep in the back.

I sincerely hoped the progress I'd made this time would not turn out like the trial or after I had had my daughter when I let the darkness take hold of me again and turn my world upside down; when I needed Judy to make it stop spinning for me so I could get back on the ladder and resume the climb – because that was what it felt like, a giant climb up from a seriously black hole. I sincerely hoped this time I'd be free of it for good. Only time would tell if it worked out that way. I read a phrase somewhere that said 'Only he who gives up is defeated'. I liked this phrase – a lot. So much so it became my new phrase. I wrote it on my bedroom wall much to the P man's dismay and right where I could see it first thing in the morning when I got out of bed. I repeated it over and over again in my head, my very own little mantra: 'Only she who gives up is defeated. Only she who gives up is defeated.' I decided I wouldn't give up and I wouldn't be defeated.

So I felt like this was it. Like this was every word of my story and there was nothing more to be added and nothing more to be gained from going over it one more time. I looked into the very depth of the darkness inside me and I poured every ounce of it into every word on every page and it was in the very *doing* of that that I would be set free.

PART FOUR

The Light

Darkness cannot drive out darkness;
only Light can do that.
Hate cannot drive out hate;
only Love can do that

> Martin Luther King Jr

Chapter Twenty-Six

I had my fire-burning ceremony in the sandstone firepit in the back garden. Over three black bin liners full of stuff went on the fire and I loved every minute of it. I burnt sage and lit loads of candles. I played trance-dancing music and rattled in the spirits asking them to help me get rid of The Terrible Tuesday completely. I drank wine and smoked while the whole lot went up in flames and it was the most fabulous experience. It truly was a magical night and I will hold it alongside all the other magical days I've had since The Terrible Tuesday – I think there are now more good days than I can count or even remember in my head. I reread and put on the fire all the cards people had sent me at the time, they were so lovely, and it was so thoughtful of everyone who sent them.

I wanted to put in just as much positive energy as I could alongside the darkness of it all and somehow restore the balance on an energetic level. I felt like I was letting it go completely and was amazed at the space in my wardrobe once it was gone. I started to leave the wardrobe door open during the day as there was nothing in there to hide any more – truly liberating. I felt like a totally different person and decided to go in a new direction. We wangled our finances (as in borrowed some more money) and I secured more time off work. My son was starting P1 in September and I was delighted I could stay at home and settle him into school properly. It was a big change from nursery and he was only just four, the youngest in the class, but he was ready for it.

I was also glad of the extended time off work as our daughter had problems with her ears and needed grommets inserted under anaesthetic. I wasn't keen on her having the operation but she had failed a couple of hearing tests and it would clear the gunge from her ears, help them drain better and improve her hearing. It was such a role reversal for me to be the parent handing over the child and not the nurse taking the child from the parent. It was a bitter pill to swallow to stand back and put her in someone else's hands for a while. It was to take twenty minutes but they didn't come for me for two hours and it was the most excruciating wait. It was easy to let fear take control of my insides, but I had to be rational and logical: it was a simple procedure and nothing would go wrong. I was so relieved to eventually hear the screams from down the corridor that signalled she was awake and raging about it all. It really improved her hearing and she got better with eating and would sleep most nights from midnight to six. It doesn't sound like much sleep but was an improvement on the past couple of years. Things were going in the right direction.

Life was fairly normal and we fell into the routine of family life. The time was right to do something for myself and I booked in to do a course in integrated energy therapy that I'd read about online. I had been reading lots of spiritual books and continuing with meditation and shamanic journeying to balance my insides. I was genuinely very happy most of the time. I had been doing a bit of spiritual work for family and friends and was ready to take it to the next stage.

The integrated energy therapy course was an eye-opener for me and I loved every minute of it. It was taught by the loveliest natural healer, a truly gifted wee lady. I found it fascinating to finally understand the effect The Terrible Tuesday had on my energy and how meditation and shamanic journeying helped heal my body, mind and soul on an energetic level. Through energy therapy you can clear the old, heavy energy that someone has held onto in their energy field, usually denoting various experiences in their life. Integrated energy therapy is a very effective form of natural healing and I liked the thought of being able to help another person feel brighter and more optimistic about their life through clearing their energy field and making room for positive new life experiences. I started practising from a makeshift workspace in the dining room on anyone who would let me. As I made my way through the three levels of integrated energy therapy, I asked the P man to turn an outside shed into a proper workspace for me so I could start seeing clients from home.

Although I had finished the training, I decided not to charge until I was a competent practitioner and could approach it with confidence instead of curiosity. Each person who came to me was a learning curve and every one surprised me with the energy they were holding onto. I enjoyed the spiritual element of healing and found it an area I had experience in. When I began working with angels, it felt very natural and normal and not at all spooky.

I never paid too much attention to angels but I believed in the afterlife. I believed our souls move into the light and I definitely believed in spirits assisting us in this lifetime. I never really thought about *why* I could see them when I was younger – the spirits or ghosts, because I thought of them with a childlike perspective. That they mostly appeared during my prayers was a good sign they were from the light and that they always told me everything would be all right was another. I didn't need to be terrified of them and none of them came to harm me in any way.

There is a dark side. I knew it to be true, and had first-hand experience of it, so why not acknowledge the light side as well? I'm pretty sure there are demons roaming the streets and very much hope there are angels around to help us and spirits around to guide us should we want their help. After The Terrible Tuesday, I'll take all the help I can get for the remainder of my time on earth. It was interesting working with angels of healing and I had a better relationship with my own guardian angel. I read a lot about angels and there was no great mystery to them. They are just non-denominational spiritual beings of light who help us in life and bridge the gap between here and heaven, so to speak.

I'd been for angel therapy a few times and was surprised by how refreshed I felt coming out – lighter, more relaxed and I always slept better for a while. With a client, I began by working on my connection with my own guardian angel, who must have thought I'd ignore her forever, and do some angel meditations to strengthen our connection. In my practice I was aiming to create a safe space for healing to occur, so I started by creating a sacred circle in which no negative entities or energies may enter. I had my little ritual of creating the space and I started the session with a few prayers for protection from Archangel Michael and the other angels of healing and asked for only the highest good and highest healing for my client throughout the session.

I asked clients to listen to a chakra-clearing meditation while I was doing the energy work. This helped them relax and meant I could focus on their energy the first time I saw them. I was realistic enough to know it wasn't possible for me to remove all the heavy energy from a person, say in their sixties, in one session, so I came to see it as a rebalancing of their energy field which went some way in helping them move forward in their life. I had faith most clients got what they needed in coming to see me, but I also knew that what they wanted and what they needed were not necessarily the same thing.

Each person had something different to say about what they experienced during their session and how they felt afterwards. Some had a profoundly spiritual experience and some just fell asleep. Deep healing can take place while asleep and I took comfort that clients were relaxed enough to sleep, and so I just tried to do my best for them while they recharged. Every single person surprised me and I loved each session because it brought up something new for me too. I could usually tell when a spirit came to assist me but it wasn't important for me to know who that spirit was.

I felt their energy when I was working as I usually worked with my eyes closed. I could normally tell if it was masculine or feminine energy and sometimes I felt them guide my hands to a spot in the client's body that needed healing. Sometimes the things I felt and heard and saw in my mind's eye didn't make sense until the end of the session and I could piece it all together, and sometimes it still didn't make sense at the end of a session but maybe it wasn't supposed to. I wish I could take credit for everything that happened inside my circles and how much lighter people felt when they left, but there were greater hands than mine at work and it would be silly not to acknowledge that. The most important part was creating a safe space for the connection to occur in the first place. The second most important part was to be balanced and happy in my own life, so I couldn't practice when the kids were sick and I wasn't getting much sleep.

I never advertised my energy work and had faith that people who needed me would find their way to me, but the most frustrating aspect was explaining to people I wasn't fortune teller or a medium. I didn't do card readings and I couldn't talk to the dead, nor would I want to. I couldn't conjure up a relative from heaven to ask them something, nor could I promise they would show up during a session. It was frustrating to constantly explain that what I provided was a healing session that may or may not be a spiritual experience for each individual, and I turned more people away than I accepted as clients.

I'd come to the end of my practice year and with my new workspace ready outside I moved my things into the den, as I called it. I was supposed to be charging people as I was totally broke but came up with a first-session-free rule to stall the process of involving money in what I did but it wasn't easy. I would have loved to offer people the same opportunity I received and I wished I were financially secure enough to do that, but the money had finally run out and I had to head back to work to pay the bills.

Patrick's mum bought a mobile home in Rossnowlagh, a popular seaside village in Donegal, and we spent all our free time there having a fabulous summer before our son started school. The kids loved the beach and the sea air helped them sleep and eat better. I walked on the beach and did yoga on it too which gave everyone a right laugh, but we were so relaxed and enjoying life. Patrick remarked on the change in me since the seventh anniversary of The Terrible Tuesday. Everything felt fresher and a bit more deep and meaningful and I told him about the new cycle and the fresh start for me. Things were going well with us although I was bitterly disappointed at having to return to community nursing and leave the children for the best part of their day. I was hoping to stay at home with them for another year but it wasn't looking likely unless I wanted to give my house back to the bank or ask my parents for more money – neither option appealed to me, so my return was scheduled for the end of January. I was quietly hoping some miracle would occur to prolong the inevitable but I was determined to enjoy the winter off and Christmas with the kids regardless.

Chapter Twenty-Seven

By the time Christmas rolled around Patrick and I were exhausted from the night-time shenanigans of our children, winter infections, the coughing and the puking and the crying, which seemed never-ending some days, plus all the bed-hopping that ensured neither of us ever got a full night's sleep. Both the children needed to get their tonsils out and our daughter needed another set of grommets, which I wasn't looking forward to, but my sister-in-law kindly agreed to look after the children again while I was at work and I was relieved they would be spending the day with someone who loved them.

I was as ready as I could be to leave the children and agreed to return to work three days a week to see how it went. The most I was hoping for was to appreciate my salary at the end of the month – the first money I'd brought home in a long time, and I was pleasantly surprised when I enjoyed my day away from home. I enjoyed the nursing and working with other people and having adult conversation that didn't revolve around my children. I found I had a lot to offer the children and families on my caseload but it soon became apparent that my little redhead hadn't taken too kindly to her mum going back to work.

My son was doing fantastically well at school and loved every minute, but his sister was up most nights and cried all the time. I arrived at work most days a complete wreck with working mother's guilt weighing so heavily upon me it was difficult to walk. I continued to pray for a miracle that would give me a bit more time at home, and after Easter in Rossnowlagh I had a terrible migraine, and for the first time in what felt like forever I told Patrick I had to lie down in the middle of the day. The rest did nothing to alleviate my headache and over the next few days I was struck down, quite literally, by the worst stomach bug I'd ever had.

I spent three days in bed and couldn't even keep water down. The poos were back, accompanied by severe vomiting, headaches, shaking and nausea. After a week I rang the doctor for medication, and after another week I went to the surgery, making the first of several trips over the coming weeks as each prescription made no difference at all. The vomiting settled but the poo kept coming and whatever I ate just ran through me. When I'd lost ten kilos and been off work for a month, I went to occupational health, saw a gastroenterologist and had to stay off work until he reviewed me and diagnosed the problem.

The irony of it all wasn't lost on me. I had continually asked to stay at home with the kids for a bit longer and my prayer was answered – although not in the way I was expecting. I was delighted God was listening but never again would I be so silly as to ask for something and not specify how I would receive it. I gave thanks to be off work and at home again, although I felt terrible letting my work colleagues down having only been back for three months. There was nothing I could do about it though. Being an infection risk meant I couldn't work with children who were already battling daily with their health, and I just had to suck it up and wait for it to settle down.

I took the opportunity to do a few more energy courses and a new course on working with the angels. I continued with my meditation and yoga which ensured I wasn't unduly stressed or anxious as I was waited for the sickness to pass. I didn't see any clients but used the den for my own healing, and the children liked to spend time out there talking about angels and God. They amazed me with their thoughts on the subject without any direction, and I'm of the firm belief that children can see and understand much more than we adults know or give them credit for. I delighted in the spiritual awareness my children naturally possessed, and even the P man had a firm belief in healing after a few spiritual experiences of his own in the den.

It seemed that when one aspect of my life settled down another aspect went spectacularly wrong, and although awaiting the next drama I was unprepared when it involved Charlie Brown, my beloved four-legged friend. He developed hip dysplasia when he was three, which affected both hips and meant he wasn't great at lead walking, preferring to swim to keep in shape, so we picnicked in the local forest park and lakes frequently so Charlie Brown could have a nice swim. The kids loved watching him glide through the water and everyone felt refreshed when we got home. There was a nice dog park near us with a river running to one side, and he often waded in there for a swim on his way round the park.

One sunny evening we headed to the park and Charlie Brown went into the water. It's separated by a fence and a steep bank, so I stayed with the children while Patrick climbed down to throw some sticks for Charlie Brown and let him have a swim. I was disturbed by a terrible feeling in my tummy, and Patrick shouted that Charlie Brown was stuck and couldn't get out of the water. He tried to get him out but he couldn't and sounded really panicked, so I made my son promise to hold onto the buggy and I made a leap over the fence and down the bank, asking the angels to please watch my children. Charlie Brown was trying to get out of the water but couldn't get himself up over the edge and Patrick told me not to go in as the current was too strong. I promptly ignored him and waded into the water lifting him out and up over the edge. I was soaked and covered in mud by the time I got him up the bank and he couldn't stand up – every time he tried his back legs went from under him and he made a terrible high-pitched sound, a wailing I'd never heard before. He reminded me of a spring lamb: every time he tried to stand up he fell over but he kept on trying and it was horrible to watch. Time had frozen as I tried to keep him calm and on the ground. When I looked up, Patrick and the children were crying.

Patrick ran back to get the jeep and I was left holding the dog. He was shaking and foaming at the mouth and was in terrible pain. Whatever had happened to his legs was really sore on him and I was terrified he wouldn't be able to walk. We got him to the vet who said his hip must have displaced in the water. He gave him an injection for the pain and said he was to rest. We were to bring him back if it happened again, but his swimming days were over and he would need regular pain relief in future. We got home and everyone was traumatised by the day's events. The children asked so many questions about Charlie Brown's sore leg that my head was spinning. He lost power in his leg twice more over the coming days and John, the vet, made a house call to see him. He said that it was time to think about

Charlie Brown's quality of life – if he couldn't walk and he couldn't swim, what would it be like for him? I was so confused and asked John exactly what he meant. He said it was time to think about the dog and not let him be in pain for my selfish reasons. Now, John had some idea of what Charlie Brown meant to me but I didn't really understand what he was suggesting. He said that Charlie Brown had done well to get to seven with such bad hips and that what had happened over the last few days was akin to him having a heart attack, the pain and pressure it put on his body, and that maybe it was time to think about letting him go, putting him to sleep with dignity and allowing him to be pain-free. I was totally speechless. I just couldn't grasp having to put him to sleep, like – forever. I couldn't do it, I just couldn't. John said to think about it and see how Charlie Brown was on his medication. I was to ring him when I was ready. Right, okay, but when John left, I had a complete meltdown. I couldn't imagine my life without Charlie Brown and I couldn't explain it to Patrick, my parents or my sister.

The next morning I headed to Rossnowlagh for a few days with the kids leaving Charlie Brown with Patrick. I couldn't look at him in pain while I thought what it meant to be without him forever. While away I mostly wondered how time went by so fast and how I thought I would have him with me for a long time to come. I thought about what I could possibly do to stall the path that led to Charlie Brown going home much sooner than I was prepared.

The sea air did much to calm my nerves and I headed home, booked an appointment with the lady who taught me the integrated energy therapy and asked her about healing animals. She told me some work had been done in America and she would get me a booklet. After reading it, I went out the back and talked to Charlie Brown. I told him I could help him with the pain and that I would like him to stay with me another while if he could. I told him he was a great dog and had been a great friend to me. I told him that if he showed me one more of those episodes where he was in pain and his legs weren't working right, then I would know he was ready to go. I made Charlie Brown a promise: I promised him I would put him to sleep as soon as he showed me he was ready.

I opened up the den and a circle of healing. Charlie Brown came in and sat at my feet. He let me put my hands on his heart centre and his hip and he sat quietly for twenty minutes while I worked before getting up and going outside. We did this a few times a week and he continued on the pain relief from the vets and showed no outward sign of being in pain. He couldn't get out much but we spent every day together and every night out the back for he loved nothing more than to sit in front of the fire with his head on my feet or being petted up beside me and Patrick, and I gave thanks to God and every angel of healing for allowing us that added time. We passed a few months like that, in suspended limbo, but I was disturbed when my dad told me the dog was done in, wrecked, and for me not to be selfish and doing him a disservice by letting him suffer – to just let him go. I told Dad I had made a deal with Charlie Brown and he would let me know when he was good and ready. I held fast to my belief that he would.

I'd always known there was a self-absorbed aspect to my recovery but it's something that couldn't be helped. It's something that has cost me dearly over the years, limiting the things I'm comfortable doing, the places I'm comfortable going and the friends I'm comfortable visiting. I tried not to focus on the limitations in my life and instead just acknowledged they were there. There are many things that made me anxious, nervous and panicky and many situations I no longer put myself in, especially the ones that put fear centre stage in my belly. I needed Charlie Brown and needed him to survive at a basic level that most people would struggle to understand. It was a difficult concept to get my head around, that I might not need him any longer.

I didn't have to wait too long anyhow, for one night I went out the back with the teapot and felt really unwell. I shook and shivered and had a terrible shooting pain down my leg. I couldn't move and thought I was going to pass out. Patrick came out and asked if I was okay, I didn't look too well, but my vision was blurry and I couldn't even answer him. I was looking around for a clear spot when I homed in on Charlie Brown – *Oh God, Patrick. It's not me. It's Charlie Brown.* Just like that, Charlie Brown fell like a ton of bricks and couldn't get up again, and just like that I was perfectly fine – although my heart was beating so loudly in my chest and I could hardly breathe because I knew, I just knew, he had allowed me to feel what he was feeling, and in that moment, when he looked in my eyes, I knew our time was up.

Chapter Twenty-Eight

I took Charlie Brown to the vet and he had another injection for the pain and a sedative to help him sleep but when we got home he couldn't sit down or get comfortable and as we settled down for the night I told Patrick I was going to sleep with our daughter. I could hear Charlie Brown crying from my bedroom and I couldn't listen to it. I went to bed with earplugs in and valiantly tried to think of a way out of keeping my promise to the dog. I didn't sleep a wink. I thought of Charlie Brown from the beginning: his grand puking entrance into my life and everything he had done for me since.

How could I explain to Patrick that Charlie Brown was my sixth sense in this world. That I could only relax because of him – that I didn't need to be on constant alert to outside danger because the dog did it for me. I knew by every movement and sound he made if I needed to be worried or not, and I knew that no one would get near me without going through him first. Every morning I let him out and up for the day and I rarely went anywhere without him. He was my sidekick, my security blanket, my one constant companion who made me feel safe in my own home and gave me the confidence to get through each day and, most especially, each night. He was my anchor in the only world I'd known since The Terrible Tuesday and I didn't think I could do it without him.

I had it all planned in my head, what I could say to Patrick that would allow me to keep Charlie Brown for a while longer, but I needn't have worried. Patrick came in at seven and had tea waiting for me. He told me he was taking the day off, that he had been outside all night with the dog and that he was ready to go. I said, 'But, Patrick.' He put his arm around me and said, 'Alana, it's time.' It was so unlike Patrick to make decisions about anything and there was little point in arguing with him – he genuinely loved Charlie Brown too, but more importantly and deep in my stomach, I knew he was right. I went to see him and he looked terrible – he was walking funny and panting and he wasn't able to hold his head up for long. His eyes were red and he just looked so sad. I opened up the den but he wouldn't walk in. He just sort of shook his head at me and walked over to the grass and lay down.

I opened my circle anyway and instead of asking for healing, I asked for strength to do what I had to do for Charlie Brown. My sister-in-law came for the kids and I told them to give Charlie Brown a hug because his leg was sore and we had to see what the vet could do for him. I didn't know when it would happen and I didn't say anything else to the children – I didn't know how to put it into words, his departure from their lives, so they both hugged him and ran off without a care in the world. We drove to the vets and Charlie Brown's legs left him in the car park but he made it up the steps. I cried making the arrangements for the vet to come to the house at two that afternoon to give Charlie Brown an injection to put him to sleep. I decided to have him cremated because I couldn't bury him in the garden in case our other dog dug him up, and this way I would have time to decide what to do with his ashes. He would go to Belfast to the small animal crematorium where he would be cremated separately so I knew that all of him would be returned to me. I didn't even ask about the price, nor did I care what it cost.

We drove home and I rang my parents. Thankfully my sister was home from Spain, so her and my mum came over before two. Patrick went to sort some stuff at work, and I was left alone with Charlie Brown in the garden for what would be the last time. I'd never really given much thought to what happened to animals after they died but I believe that every living thing has a spirit and that their spirit leaves their body upon death. I didn't know if Charlie Brown's spirit would go to heaven as I knew it, but I'd come to see heaven as a realm of incredible love and light and I was sure there was a place in it for my beloved friend. I did all I could to help him on his way for he deserved an afterlife of green fields and sunshine and all the swimming in the world. I wanted to do all I could to make that happen for him. I opened a circle around our lawn, the spot he would pick to breathe his last, and placed my candles and incense. I gathered together all the angels and saints, all my spirit guides and guardians, and my family and friends in the sky and asked them to come together today to welcome a great friend of mine who did me a great service in his lifetime and deserved to be rewarded with every good thing the afterlife had to offer him.

Charlie Brown walked around after me. I felt he knew I was preparing the way for him and he was helping me in my endeavours. I made him bacon sandwiches and tried to calm the knot in my stomach as we waited for the vet to arrive. I felt like I couldn't breathe properly but I was determined to hold it together for him because it was the right thing to do. I brushed him, cleaned his teeth and his ears and Patrick arrived home, closely followed by Mum and my sister. Lastly, the vet arrived, and suddenly, it was time.

The vet brought a young girl on work experience with her. I told the vet it wasn't a good idea for her to be there. I know some people are okay with putting their dogs to sleep, but I wasn't that person and it was going to be horrendous. She told me she would be fine and not to worry. I asked my sister to help me send his spirit skyward in case I couldn't do it once he was gone. The vet gave him a sedative but he didn't need it. Charlie Brown greeted the vet warmly and gave her his paw as if he knew what was coming. He walked around for a minute or two and then came back and lay down on the grass. Patrick and I were both talking and petting him and he put his head on my legs and closed his eyes when she gave him the injection. He took a couple of deep breaths and then no more.

I felt him move past me though I was stuck in the moment waiting for him to breathe again even when I knew he was gone. There was a stillness in him and a pain in my chest so heavy I couldn't breathe. I couldn't get enough air into my lungs and I thought I was going to pass out. I looked at Mum and my sister and they were both crying. From their expressions they knew the meltdown was coming as I started a terrible wailing and crying. No matter how hard I cried I couldn't get it past the pain in my chest, and I looked to my mummy to help me with it. I couldn't move from the grass and I couldn't believe he was gone. Patrick tried to comfort me but it was no use, and I didn't want to be comforted anyway. I don't know how long I lay on the grass holding his head and just crying. It was excruciatingly painful and everyone was distraught.

My sister began the process of sending his spirit skyward and I knew I had to get up and do it myself. I had to honour him in that way or I would regret it forever. The young girl with the vet was taken out to the car she was so upset, so I had a bit of time to send all the love I had for him in my heart skyward too, in case it would send his spirit home faster and ease his passing. I told Patrick to let our other dog out and I told her to come and say goodbye to Charlie Brown. She came over at a snail's pace and sniffed and licked him before burying her head in my side. She couldn't look at him so lifeless on the grass.

All the spiritual assistance in the universe couldn't ease this for me, and all I wanted to do was go back in time and not give him the fucking injection. The vet came back with a sheet to wrap Charlie Brown in and I was enraged it was so dirty and full of holes. 'Jesus,' I said, 'I am not putting him in that,' and I got one from the cupboard and wrapped him myself. Patrick and I carried him out to the car and placed him on the back seat. It was over. The vet drove away with my most treasured possession on her back seat and I stood there watching the lane long after they were gone.

The next few days were atrocious. I felt like I had returned to the vacant place in my head in trying to move away from the pain of losing Charlie Brown. I could hardly muster up the energy to speak and cried non-stop – really cried, where I had no control over how loud it was or how to stop. There was a quietness out the back that I wouldn't have believed possible before his departure. Even the air felt still and oppressive, and every time I went out there I couldn't breathe properly and my stomach was in tatters. Our other dog sat at the gate and didn't eat a bite or make a sound for three days.

The children were enraged and our daughter looked for him constantly, calling his name and barking so he would hear her and come back. Our son was particularly upset and told me it was my fault Charlie Brown was gone; that if I hadn't agreed to let him go then he would still be here; that when the angels came for him I should've done a Spiderman jump on him and kept him. There was nothing I could say to the children to help them feel better and they were too young to understand the nature of death, but the truth in my son's statement surprised me. He had it correct when he said Charlie Brown would still be with us if I hadn't agreed to let him go, so I tried to explain that it was better for Charlie Brown but they didn't understand and were angry with me as well as being genuinely sad for the first time in their little lives. We read a little book about water bugs and dragonflies that helped explain heaven and life after death but it was a confusing and sad time for them.

A couple of days later I walked into the kitchen to find one of my friends sitting at the table with a bunch of flowers. I instantly started crying and wailing. She was horrified and I had trouble explaining that it wasn't her presence that upset me. It was because I didn't hear her come in, and for the first time in almost eight years Charlie Brown wasn't there to tell me someone was at the gate, nor did he come round to see who it was and alert me to any possible stranger danger. It was the first time I truly appreciated how my life would change without him and the sadness was overwhelming.

The fear returned to my belly. A couple of days later a guy from NIE came to the door and I had to let him in to read the meter. I couldn't get the door open my hands were shaking so much and I seriously thought I was heading straight into meltdown city. Only the centre was closed I probably would have hightailed it back to therapy. I could get hold of Judy if I really wanted to but the rational part of my mind kept reminding me it was grief – in all its wonderful glory – and it mattered not that he was only a dog.

So instead I concentrated on remaining calm and religiously meditating and taking myself out to the den for a spot of self-healing whenever the opportunity presented itself. Charlie Brown's ashes arrived at the vet's and I was pleasantly surprised by the way they were presented and the accompanying poem, 'The Rainbow Bridge', which gave me great comfort. I put them out in the den while I worked out what to do with them. I prayed constantly for the strength to get through my grief and the strength to stay out of the darkness but I knew I would just have to work through it.

It was unbelievably painful and seemed to hit me in waves of extreme emotion. It wasn't just the loss of the dog I was grieving for, it was the loss of a whole way of life for me. A life that I painstakingly built around myself after The Terrible Tuesday; one I felt safe enough in to live pretty normally without giving in to fear all the time. I was unsure of what the next chapter held for me and of how I was going to be but I reminded myself that the time was right for Charlie Brown's departure and I mustn't need him any more to move forward.

During one of my meditations, I had an out-of-body experience when the wind took me to the upper world and I was in a green meadow that seemed to go on for miles. I couldn't see anything or anyone, so I sat quietly and waited, and then I heard him bounding towards me like a racehorse and I saw him running and I was so happy he was okay and I cried on the bed in my den. I petted him and talked to him and I heard in my head that it didn't matter what I did with his ashes for I would carry him in my heart always – but that his favourite place was the lakes where he loved to swim.

Right in front of my eyes, he changed into a ball of golden light and became smaller and smaller until he fitted perfectly within my heart. His light strengthened me and made my own light stronger and brighter. When I opened my eyes the meditation had finished and I was still crying but comforted in the knowledge that Charlie Brown had made it to his afterlife. The experience, as a whole, strengthened me rather than broke me, which I was seriously worried about, but the pain in my chest didn't leave and I carried the loss heavily within me. I began to do the things I would have done with him, and the first task was to take his ashes to the lakes and spread some in the water, and then put the rest around the roots of a flowering crab apple tree and have Patrick plant it overlooking the lake. It was a fitting final resting place for him and it would flower and grow and get stronger every year – a testament to him and his gift to me.

Adjusting to life without him was more difficult than I imagined, and Patrick and I discussed the possibility of moving house. We had talked about it many times but always thought he would be coming with us, and honestly I was loathe to leave my little cottage and all the memories it held for us, never mind the safety and security I felt at living so close to my brother, but I knew we needed more space and it was a good time to sell.

Over the coming months I found it hard to find any peace without Charlie Brown. Everything felt so challenging that I wondered if a new house would really make it any worse for me than it already was. I was already on a new path and was daily shedding most of my homemade security measures. Maybe it was time to dive in again instead of just wetting my toes. I'd never been one for half measures, and if I could survive without Charlie Brown then I could survive a new house too.

The decision made, we prepared the house for going on the market. The time had also come for me to return to work. The gastroenterologist had had a look at my stomach and he thought I had a particularly nasty case of food poisoning which had destroyed the lining of my stomach and duodenum giving me a hard time digesting dairy products. The pain and poo would settle if I avoided dairy, and I laughed at the irony – I had now joined in solidarity with my non-dairy-eating children. Although I'd seriously miss pizza, I was relieved it was nothing too serious and the end was in sight.

I attended a few sessions of integrated energy therapy and angel healing to help with my grief and sadness and to prepare me for the challenges ahead: returning to the madness of full-time nursing with two young children, and preparing to leave my lovely little cottage – the setting of much of my recovery since The Terrible Tuesday. I was still feeling quite wobbly after Charlie Brown's death – maybe I had taken on too many challenges at the one time. I feared leaving my brother could be the most painful part of my new endeavour and resolved to take one day at a time. I would need all the help I could get, so I increased my praying and asked for serious assistance on the road ahead.

Chapter Twenty-Nine

My return to work went much smoother this time round, although my daughter took every opportunity she could to complain and saved every tantrum and tear for my return home spending the couple of hours we had together making me pay for my absence. My sister-in-law assured me she was happy and content as soon as I left her off – a model child until I picked her up again, and I felt so guilty at leaving her that maybe I deserved it for being an absentee mother. She kicked and screamed and created havoc in the house until Patrick and I were at breaking point and we shouted at each other, both of us firmly believing the other was in the wrong.

My days were never-ending with all the chores to be done in the evening and so much organising for the next day. I resented Patrick for his continuing lack of contribution towards all the domestic crap that ate into any free time I had for myself – he wasn't even aware of half the work I did in the house to keep everything running smoothly. The laundry fairy left his clean clothes on the bed, his dinner magically in front of him in the evenings and magically replenished cupboards overnight as well as being magically able to complete about ten tasks at once and not forget a thing.

Communication wasn't our strong point and we were constantly exhausted and angry at each other for some reason or another. He told me not to complain for doing what all mothers do every day of the week, and I thought being my soulmate was about all he had going for him some days. I continually wanted to punch him for being no help to me whatsoever. We finally sat down to delegate the tasks out more evenly between the two of us, which went some way to making me feel we were a partnership rather than me being a maid all the time. It took a while but eventually I felt more settled in the routine of going to work every day and continued to remind myself I had no choice: we needed the money and I had to work. End of story.

It didn't take long before I was enjoying work. My caseload was busy and full of children with complex needs whose families faced challenges far greater than mine. I should have felt grateful for my daughter's ability to scream the house down in bad temper when I got home instead of worrying about it all the time. I still felt emotionally vulnerable after Charlie Brown's death, and was unsure how I would feel when having to care for a dying child and their family at work. It would be my first experience dealing with that aspect of nursing since having my daughter whose frequent bouts of sickness and hospitalisations changed my perspective, and to be honest I didn't know how I would cope with the horror of it when it came calling.

I hadn't had time to see anyone in my den and instead thought of my nursing as a form of healing too; one I had to concentrate on for now because I'd been off for so long I needed to get up to speed with all the changes in practice. Most days I was too busy to dwell on how well I was or wasn't managing things, but I felt under so much pressure all the time and had so many balls in the air that I couldn't stop juggling, even for a second, and I was so saddened to realise I had done what I promised myself I wouldn't do after The Terrible Tuesday: I had, once again, joined the rat race where I was so busy I didn't have time to enjoy my life and I spent far too much time doing things I didn't enjoy. The saddest thing was that the children had to stick to my mental schedule instead of the nice daily routine we had going, and I just barked orders at them all the time to get them to move within my time frame.

I was back at it a couple of months when I gradually increased my hours to full-time, which gave me even less time at home. I was still working in a neighbouring county, so most days I left around eight fifteen in the morning and rocked home any time after six in the evening. I worked every third weekend as well, so I spent more time at work than I did at home with the kids and the guilt was pretty tough to take. It made me miserable on the inside and it didn't take long for my mood to slip and for me to feel pretty bleak. Patrick told me to catch myself on, the children were perfectly happy, and it was a sad fact of life that most families couldn't survive on one wage, especially as his work is seasonal. He was raised by a working mother, it didn't do him any harm and I would just have to suck it up. But my mum was at home with us and I had such fond memories of being at home after school and her helping with homework and reading to us, and I always felt safe that she was at home and I was sad I was unable to do that for my own children.

In the middle of it all we put the house on the market and it was sale agreed quickly only to fall through when we couldn't find anywhere suitable to move into. I disliked most houses we saw, irrationally because they weren't the cottage, and Patrick told me to catch myself on again when I tried to have a say in who bought the cottage despite the offer they made on it. I knew he didn't understand that it was important to me who I gave my cottage to, but I wanted it to go to someone who would genuinely love it as much as I had done.

The cottage had a lovely peaceful feel to it and great energy within it. It had been a little oasis of calm for me while I licked my wounds after The Terrible Tuesday, and I wanted it to go to someone who would appreciate the space and what it had to offer. I was overruled when it came to the crunch and we accepted the next offer that was made. We found a house to rent not too far away and agreed a date to move. The packing commenced, and at the same time a job came up in my local area which would save me a lot of travelling, so I swotted for a job interview, my first in years, and packed at the same time.

After much delay, interview day finally dawned, and loaded down with crystals I drove to the local hospital to get it over and done with. I was ridiculously nervous although well prepared, and once I got into the swing of it, it went all right. The trust's interview process is so formal and my nerves ensured I forgot half the stuff I'd read before I entered the room, but I must have answered well because they offered me the job later that day and I accepted with delight and relief that I would be working closer to home and would be able to take the children to school in the mornings and help settle my daughter into nursery in September.

It had taken me almost nine years to get back to the same band in nursing that I was when I worked in London. The road had been long and unyielding at times but I felt ready to accept the challenges a senior post had to offer and I knew that the time was right. The delay wasn't solely down to The Terrible Tuesday, having babies derailed me professionally for a couple of years too, but I was ridiculously pleased to have done well in the interview and was looking forward to starting my new post.

We had the summer to pack up and move house prior to starting nursery and my new job, and of course because things had been going well and according to plan for a change, it was a shock for everyone when Patrick became unwell. He had been having what his GP termed stress-induced migraines for quite some time now – something which brought him much more sleep than I could ever have hoped to have, but, on a serious note, he felt nauseous, dizzy, shaky and faint. His colour would change dramatically and he would almost pass out and have a severe headache. I didn't witness the first few episodes, but on my return from one of our daughter's many trips to the hospital for intravenous fluids, he had a mammoth one which scared the life out of me. I had put our son in the bath and asked Patrick to feed our daughter. He called me to the living room as she had projectile vomited everywhere, and her brother was shouting from the bathroom that he had to poo. I took her to the bathroom with me to discover a bath full of diarrhoea – the bath full of toys, I might add, so I let the water out and went back to tell Patrick about the poo. He was trying to clean the vomit from the living room floor, retching while he was at it, and all of a sudden said he didn't feel well and collapsed onto the floor. I made sure he was breathing and stepped round him and the vomit to get the phone. I phoned Mum, and once she answered I could hardly tell her what had happened for laughing. I laughed so much she was seriously concerned but I couldn't help it. Eventually I managed to tell her I needed her to come and help me – there was a bath full of diarrhoea, a living room full of vomit, two very dirty and wet children and to top it all off Patrick was passed out on the floor and he needed to go to the doctor. She asked if I was all right and I said that if I didn't laugh about it, I might just down tools, get into my car, drive off and just keep on driving.

Mum came and helped me sort it out, and Patrick came back from the doctors with his diagnosis of stress-induced migraines, and after me not having had one wink of sleep for the last three days, Patrick had to go to bed and rest for a couple of days. The rest didn't seem to help him much and not long after another spectacular episode I did some healing on his heart centre. When my hands became very cold I said enough was enough and frogmarched him over to the cardiac assessment unit at the hospital.

Patrick wasn't best pleased but as soon as they hooked him up to monitors I could see his heart wasn't beating in a normal rhythm, and it was no surprise he had to stay in for further investigation. He came home attached to a heart monitor and slept a lot. He was very quiet and I didn't say too much – too terrified that there might be something really wrong with him, and what I would do if he weren't here. I just tried to do everything in the normal way and not let on that I was seriously panicking about his heart.

I got a phone call from our son's teacher asking if everything was all right at home as he'd been very emotional and upset. I was gutted to realise I had been so wrapped up in my own fears that I hadn't even thought about how it was affecting the children. I was so sad when our son asked if his daddy was going to heaven to be with Charlie Brown because his daddy was sick and that's what happened to Charlie Brown when he got sick. I tried to answer honestly and explained that everyone goes to heaven eventually but Daddy wasn't going anywhere for a long time. I hoped and prayed that was the truth and I hadn't just told the biggest lie in the world to my son who would never forgive me if I was wrong.

Lots of tests later we discovered Patrick had a condition called atrial fibrillation; his heart doesn't beat in the normal rhythm – it skips a beat or beats too fast, and that daily medication and a stress-free existence should keep it under control. Easier said than done but we had to try. We were relieved that it was nothing more serious, but it was apparent that a couple of years of no sleep and lots of pressure has taken its toll on Patrick's body. He was exhausted. I was exhausted at the thought of what lay ahead: packing the entire contents of our cottage, almost single-handedly as Patrick was busy at work and so tired in the evening I couldn't ask him to help, and leaving it behind. My stomach was jam-packed with nervous anxiety about everything in my life – moving house and leaving my brother, starting my new job, our daughter going to nursery and Patrick's bloody heart condition. And God, I could cry when I thought about missing Charlie Brown.

There was nothing else for it but to keep moving through it. Keep doing what I had to do every day and keep pushing through all the dark, heavy stuff with the goal always in mind: don't give up and I would never be defeated. So I kept meditating, kept going to work, kept running the house and looking after the children and kept packing boxes. Eventually it was done, there wasn't one other thing to pack and not one box left in the cottage.

My den had become the storage area for all the boxes, and the cottage looked as empty as it could be with people still in it. I tried valiantly not to panic too much at leaving it behind me. As the moving date drew closer, my anxiety levels were at an all-time high. I went for some energy therapy and angel healing and it calmed my nerves a bit and put things in perspective. We were moving because we needed more space and I no longer needed all my self-built security measures for survival. Everything would work out perfectly fine if I remained calm and balanced and in a receptive state. There was no need to panic, and I was reassured I was on the right path and everything was in order. Everything was organised and my parents took the kids for the weekend to allow us to move between the two houses. My brother had gone away for the weekend which made it easier not to cry too much, so we got on with loading up the vehicles and saying goodbye to the cottage.

It was a mad couple of days but pretty soon the cottage was completely empty and I walked around it room by room thinking of all the wonderful memories we made within those walls. All the birthday parties, Christmas Eve parties and the outside parties, every milestone the children reached and how much happiness and love we all experienced here. I thought about the endless nights of crying, the puking and the patience of Charlie Brown in waiting his turn for a bit of attention when there weren't enough hours in the day for me, and how happy I was to have had him with me all that time.

I thanked the spirit of the cottage graciously for keeping me so safe and secure and I was very emotional when I finished cleaning it and closed the door for the last time. Patrick and the kids were super excited about the new house, the space, the garden, the treehouse, everything about the new property, but I found it hard to share in their excitement.

Chapter Thirty

Although still close to town, it felt like we had moved to the middle of nowhere. The first thing that unnerved me was the darkness. From early evening it was pitch black outside, you couldn't see in front of yourself and there were no neighbours close enough to see any other house lights. Being used to seeing right into my brother's living room when I looked out the windows, it was a challenge to get comfortable in the dark and the space.

My mind ran through all the possibilities for disaster, all the terrible things that could happen without Charlie Brown and my brother to hand, and it was exhausting to continually hold my nerve every time a strange car pulled up or someone came to the door. The house itself was old and creaky and made noises as the heat settled. I was jumpy and anxious with every noise that I couldn't rationally explain. I was up and down like a yo-yo at night checking things out, and Patrick was angry and impatient with me. After a few weeks I didn't even wake him any more, and he had no idea why I was so grumpy in the mornings or how little sleep I got at night.

The chances of a repeat experience were slim, of course I understood that logically, but my mind reminded me of the other time I ignored noises that were unfamiliar while I was sleeping in bed, and the consequences were so horrific that I continued my nightly rounds of checking things and looking out windows into the pitch-black night hoping that there was nothing out there intending to harm me or my children.

The children loved everything about it. They loved the garden and spending time outdoors and Patrick loved it too. I was alone in my anxiety and my inability to relax in my new surroundings. I had no space to meditate or do my shamanic work and no time for yoga I was so busy with my new job and day-to-day life. I forgot how important those practices were for my mental health, and everything took a nosedive downwards and filled me with despair. The only thing I had time to continue with before I fell into bed was my reading, and even that led me further down a dark road when I came across some work by an Irish faith healer who said that my spiritual practices, and even my yoga, were offensive to God, satanic in nature and that I needed to hightail it back to Mass and beg forgiveness for worshipping the devil. I was unsettled in my head and my belly and thought I was having a spiritual crisis. I had out-of-body experiences and scary dreams and unpleasant visions, and I didn't know which direction to move forward in. I wished with all my heart I could have an honest-to-God conversation with Judy about everything that was going horribly wrong, and I tried to think about what she would say to me that would help me pick myself up and get me off the road to no town which was where I was headed.

I thought back to our previous conversations and realised that I didn't rock up to our sessions and listen while she gave me the answer to every problem I had or every challenge I was facing. No, that wasn't how it worked. Mostly Judy listened while I talked through every problem or challenge, and while she certainly guided me in the right direction I worked hard at finding a way forward myself. I actually had all the tools necessary to work out the way forward myself, and I realised it was time to gather myself together and resume the climb. Feeling sorry for myself was getting me nowhere.

The first thing on my new to-do list was to sort myself out spiritually, for that would eventually manifest itself physically, and while I had been connecting with my spirit guides and angel guardians for a long time now, I thought the time had come to go directly to the man himself. I rocked up to chapel, took a seat and said, 'Hello, God, it's me, Margaret,' and had a little chuckle about how witty I was. On a serious note I said, 'Hello, God, it's me, Alana,' and proceeded to have a one-sided conversation where I got no answers but at least felt like he was listening. I apologised for causing offence as that was not my intention, and explained that I was under the impression he was within me and all around me, that it mattered not how or where I worshipped, only that I did worship, and that if my intention was pure in my heart, then anything was possible.

I felt a connection, a closeness, to God through my spiritual practice and work with energy and the angels, and explained that these were the tools I'd used in my recovery and that I had to take my chances that this was the way to move forward because I didn't feel right without them. I felt an affinity with nature and the shamanic way of thinking, feeling and doing, and I didn't think it would benefit me to change direction now. I promised to make more of an effort in my direct relationship with him while keeping in mind to always lead a life full of love and light and work through periods of darkness with faith instead of doubt and fear.

I resumed my meditations with relief and booked myself in for some integrated energy therapy to begin clearing my energy field and moving the fear out of my belly. I went to confessions and Mass to cement my new commitment, and my mother was relieved not to have any more in-depth spiritual discussions with me for of late I had exhausted her with my questions about God and the devil and what it meant in the grand scheme of things. I immediately felt a lot lighter and had a brighter, more optimistic outlook.

While out for a drive we came across a property, not far from where we were living, that I feel drawn towards. I made Patrick stop the car and got out so I could have a proper look. The house was built and the roof was on but that was it. It was clearly unfinished. It sat behind some trees and the outside was a complete mess, but I instantly loved it and was disappointed but not undeterred when I couldn't find a 'For Sale' sign anywhere on the property. I made Patrick pull in to the next house and asked the owner about the property: yes, it was his and, no, it wasn't for sale. I gave him my number, told him we were interested in buying the house and finishing it and asked him to call me if he wanted to discuss it.

Patrick thought I was mad but I felt it in my stomach that it was right for us and I wouldn't ignore my feelings. The owner agreed to sell and we agreed the price. I set about finding the finance to fund the project amidst lots of doubt and speculation whether it was the right way forward. Financing the project turned out to be more complicated than I thought and I was on the verge of giving up but this time Patrick held fast and firm that it was right for us and it was with relief that our cottage sale finally went through and we were able to purchase the shell of what would be our forever home.

Patrick and I discussed finishing the property but disagreed over every small detail – so much so that my head was wrecked with it all before it had even begun and I thought we might just continue to constantly fight and bicker with each other for the foreseeable future. I wasn't sure we would survive much more fighting and resolved to look at things between us and at home objectively with a plan for improvement. Our daughter hadn't settled into nursery the way her brother had and her tantrums were getting increasingly worse as the year went on. She was angry and enraged and she screamed and cried at some point almost every day, creating such tension and anger between Patrick and me as we tried to figure out how to deal with her meltdowns, unsuccessfully most of the time, and even every *Supernanny* trick in the book didn't seem to work, and, again, we were at a loss as to how to help her.

The only successful trick we had was to phone her granddad who could usually talk her down within minutes, but we tried everything else before giving in and picking up the phone. Sometimes even then she kept it up for hours and made herself hoarse from all the screaming and sick from retching, and I totally despaired to see her so upset, usually over something insignificant. Patrick and I were both struggling to deal with it. The terrible twos ran into the terrible threes and became the terrible fours, and it was with a heavy heart that I admitted we needed help and phoned her consultant.

After an endoscope we discovered she hadn't grown out of her reflux or her allergies and continued to need medication and careful monitoring of her diet, and, yes, the hospitalisations and sickness could be contributing to her behavioural issues, but there were also worrying patterns of behaviour and when he mentioned the autistic spectrum I nearly fell off my chair with shock and immediately felt so stupid for not connecting the dots myself. He was to organise some investigations and I went home and gave myself a stern talking to: I wouldn't allow myself to have a meltdown.

I read and read around the subject and equipped myself with knowledge and then I made a plan. I wasn't surprised to discover that in a lot of cases effective parenting could improve the situation dramatically, and I was ready to admit that Patrick and I had never been on the same parenting page. We had dramatically different upbringings and both brought different skills to the table. Neither of us had a clue what to do with our wee redhead, but before we allowed her to be labelled permanently, we had to work together and give her every opportunity to grow and develop in a positive way.

I made Patrick read lots around discipline and setting boundaries and being consistent with our approach and not giving her an opportunity to divide and conquer, which she had skilfully been doing for a long time now – which made me incredibly proud of how clever she was and how strong she was in spirit but which I thought could be put to better use than screaming the house down to get what she wanted. I told Patrick we were going for couples therapy and I didn't give him the opportunity to say no – it was non-negotiable. We had to have a safe space to discuss the challenges of parenting and setting ground rules for the future of our relationship and our family. Patrick wasn't too impressed with my plan but I wasn't a stay-at-home mum. We both worked full-time and I was unmoved in my resolve that parenting should be a shared responsibility. To modify our daughter's behaviour, we both needed to be on board with every aspect of the plan. I needed his support in managing her challenging behaviour if were to see any improvement.

We made some family rules, all of us together at the kitchen table, and outlined the plan for discipline if the rules were broken. It didn't take long for us to become exhausted from the pressure of hanging in there, but we were happy that we stuck to the plan, and I thought now was as good a time as any to tell Patrick I thought we should get another dog. He looked at me with a you-are-not-serious face, but I calmly explained that everyone missed Charlie Brown, not just me. It had been over a year since his death and the kids still talked about him. My sleeping pattern hadn't improved and I missed the safety of having a big animal outside. Our family missed the routine of caring for a big dog – the walks and swims and picnics that gave us more of a focus, and I thought it would be good for our daughter.

I could survive without another big dog, but I didn't want to. I missed Charlie Brown dreadfully and I knew another dog wouldn't replace him but I missed walking too. I didn't have the confidence to go out on the country roads on my own, especially in the evenings which was the only time I actually had the time to go. Patrick said no. It wasn't the time for another addition to the family, we were under enough bloody pressure with the new house, and after some arguing about it I said fine, but quietly asked the angels to help with my request and left it at that.

Chapter Thirty-One

I tried to put the idea out of my head and not keep harping on at Patrick, but I registered with the local animal shelter, knowing he would see the pictures of the dogs in our area that needed rehomed on my newsfeed as he spent a fair amount of time on Facebook sorting out his business page. I knew it would take time for him to come round to the idea, but I was prepared to wait until he agreed with me. I envisioned telling the kids we had a surprise for them and the happiness we would all feel when we brought home our new dog. I kept that vision in my mind at all times while quietly telling myself it was only a matter of time before I would get a good night's sleep.

I was so busy over the winter with work and dealing with the kids' continual infections and the ongoing lack of sleep that the new dog idea quickly took a back seat to my more pressing issues. Two of the children on my caseload came to the end of their road on earth and it was with nervous trepidation that we tried to support the families through the most difficult of times. The first one was a little girl who I had looked after for years and who I genuinely loved with all my heart. It had been a long time since I'd made such a deep connection with one of my children at work and I couldn't explain how I allowed it to happen except to say that I couldn't help it.

She was a beautiful little girl with a wicked sense of humour who made me smile and laugh and whose heart was wide open, loving nothing more than to give love and be loved in return. I always knew her time here would be short. Her suffering was so great and she bore it so well and with such courage and bravery that I was in awe of her and respected her enormously. I just knew in my heart she wouldn't have to do it for long. I stopped looking after her on a daily basis when I started my new job – only covering her area at weekends and if they were short-staffed, so I stupidly assumed this gradual withdrawal from nursing her would ease her passing for me. I kept in touch with her mum and called in to see her when I could but I was only a couple of months into my new job when her care became palliative.

They decided to stay in the local children's unit, so my role was only to support the family and wasn't one of clinical nursing, something which caused me great relief. I was upset enough about her passing without trying to hold it together and be a professional at the same time. I felt compelled to visit her one evening and drove down to the hospital in the snow, arriving just as everyone else was leaving. I got to spend a few precious hours with her on my knee, singing and talking, and this sentence kept repeating itself over and over in my mind: 'There but for the grace of God go I,' and despite the heavy sedation she opened her eyes and lifted her hand to my face and I knew she was saying goodbye.

I was struck by how beautiful she was. How small she really was when I held her in my arms, and considering the massive impact she had on everyone she met I was struck by how young she was when she always seemed so wise. Eight years isn't a long life by any stretch, but it depends on how you see it. Eight years of living with a debilitating and painful disease is way too long, and some people won't have given or received the love she did in eighty years never mind eight, and for that alone she should be airlifted straight to heaven in front of our very eyes.

The sadness of her death was overwhelming, and I was struck again by how little I really understood about life except to say that some days are excruciating and feel almost impossible to get through. Within a couple of days, another little eight-year-old, a boy this time, had come home to die following a long and courageous battle with cancer. My colleagues and I rallied round providing round-the-clock nursing so his family could keep him at home in his final hours. This too was excruciating on my already weakened spirit. That boy held a special place in my heart because I cared for him a lot throughout his treatment and he, too, warmed my heart with his kindness and strength. It was a difficult time and we were all exhausted when it was over, and I was emotionally wrecked and beyond sad, but on top of that the fear was back in my belly, which often happened when I took my eye off the ball, so to speak. Every time I went home I was terrified something would happen to my own children, and I worried about it all the time. Normal every day childhood illnesses took on a whole new meaning for me and in my mind I went through all the potential opportunities for disaster.

The thought of saying goodbye to my own children scared the life out of me and I prayed constantly for their safety, protection and health. Having witnessed the devastation of a family unit at the death of a child, I didn't think it was something I could pull myself through and all of a sudden I was grateful, once again, for The Terrible Tuesday. I continually returned to feeling grateful once I'd worked my way through a challenging period in my life, and this time I'd managed to work my way through it without the help of Judy or therapy. I was and hoped, and prayed, to remain ever grateful that my worst day didn't include one of my children.

Whatever way I looked at it, The Terrible Tuesday would always remain one of my worst days ever and short of losing one of my children, Patrick or another family member in some dreadful twist of fate, it was bound to hold the top spot for some time to come. I resigned myself to this sad fact on the understanding that it couldn't be undone. All I could change was how I felt about it and how I lived my life because of it. The last few months in work had shown me it was time to go in another direction. I had faced enough death, devastation, despair and loss to last me a lifetime and I knew my personal experience brought a depth to my nursing that wasn't there before, just as being a mummy brought a depth of understanding to the loss of a child that I didn't have working in London. I now thought that rock bottom was the same awful place for everyone, regardless of how you got there. It mattered not whether it was trauma or grief or some other godawful experience that pulled the rug from beneath you and landed you at the bottom. All that mattered was that you got yourself back up again. Frontline nursing with dying children took so much of my energy and left me feeling so sad on the inside, so super anxious all the time about my own children, that it wasn't good for me to continue doing it every day.

I had been working with sick children for twenty years and I knew I needed to use my experience to move forward but leave the end-of-life care behind me. I hadn't yet worked out the details of how my nursing career would move on, but I asked God and the angels to make the path ahead clearer for me and I had faith that they would do. My energy levels had increased since making my decision and my anxiety levels were a bit steadier now I knew in my heart I wouldn't be doing it forever.

It was the tenth anniversary of The Terrible Tuesday, and I couldn't believe how time had gone and all the changes in my life over the last ten years. I had come so far down the road that it pained me to look back at to the very beginning. Some days it felt like it was every day of the ten years behind me and some days it felt like yesterday, with no correlation to how I felt about it except that it very much depended on the time of year and what was going on inside my own head.

Every summer my sleep pattern took a nosedive, complicated by the Charlie Brown situation and moving house, yes, but also by my anxiety levels and disturbing dreams that I couldn't quite put my finger on. I no longer dreamt of Him or any aspect of The Terrible Tuesday – the fear seemingly in experiences that lay ahead of me rather than behind. My body valiantly tried to remember why it was so anxious and tried to drag memories up from the recesses of my mind but it was no longer possible. I had made peace with my memories in my head and my heart and they no longer had the power to hurt me.

My reading led me to thinking about forgiveness over the last few years. Initially it began as a very loose concept in my mind. Forgiveness, as in forgiving Him and letting it go completely, was a tall order to even consider in the beginning, but I thought about it in terms of severing whatever connection I had with Him to start with. If I didn't try to forgive Him on some level and instead held onto it in my insides, what good would that do me in the long run and did it mean my healing would never be complete? Did it mean the whole experience could come around again to haunt me or my children? There was no one who could answer my questions and it was one of those situations I could never really be sure of, so I would just have to give it a go to be on the safe side of never allowing it to happen again.

I went for a few sessions of integrated energy therapy and angel healing and initially began by forgiving myself for ever intentionally or unintentionally causing harm to myself or others before working on forgiving others for any harm caused to me. I didn't single Him out in my work, and in the beginning I wasn't even sure I meant it, but by continually working on it and meditating around it I hoped it would slowly dissolve whatever was left on my insides because of Him and His terrible actions towards me on that dreadful morning and every other challenging moment I'd had since then. Honestly, it was a work in progress, and I was unsure if I would ever achieve it but it was one I wouldn't give up on and one which won't defeat me. Was He still in prison and had He changed at all?

It was no surprise that Rachel invited me to London for her daddy's eightieth birthday party that just happened to fall on the weekend of the tenth anniversary of The Terrible Tuesday. I hadn't returned to London since the trial ended, had never returned the friendship so kindly bestowed on me by Rachel and I very much wanted to visit her and go to the party. I thought the timing couldn't be any worse and then I thought the timing was exactly right. I decided I would go and visit Rachel and catch up with her daddy. It was time to lay all the old ghosts to rest, and I decided to see if I could catch up with Julie and John and maybe swing by the flat and visit the nuns while I was there, and if I could, that there was a much more important visit, than going on a trip down memory lane.

Should I contact Phil to see if he fancied meeting up for a coffee? It had been such a long time, but I was and always would be a bit disturbed by how our relationship ended, and if we lived in the same country we would have met up a long time ago. The only stumbling block was whether he wanted to meet me. I ran it past Patrick before I made any firm plans with Rachel or Phil and, no, he didn't want to come with me and, no, he had no issue with my weekend plans or with me meeting up with Phil. It was all systems go.

I booked my flights and asked my sister to come from Spain and meet me. I was under no illusion how difficult I might find it all and I needed some support. She readily agreed, but once decided I began to think that maybe I was mad putting myself under so much pressure in returning to the scene of crime. Then I reminded myself how far I had come since that fateful day and how it would be a great achievement to have faced it all again and closed the door on it once and for all. I was reminded of my vow in the beginning: when I was told the trial would be within a year, I gave Him one year of my life before I would put it all behind me. I laughed at how naive I was back then to think that a year would even begin to scratch the surface of my recovery.

How I thought I could begin to understand how long that road was when I wasn't altogether there was beyond me, but I was grateful for that too; that sincere lack of knowledge and understanding of what lay ahead of me and for Judy's gentle philosophy of dealing with one day at a time and only doing what I felt I could cope with on any given day. I looked back at the limitations in my life since The Terrible Tuesday and realised I had pushed my way through a lot of challenges but there was one that remained outstanding and on the back-burner for years: the dentist.

I made an appointment and it was with horror and dread that I sat in the chair and was told I would need eight fillings and a wisdom tooth extraction. Sweet holy mother of God, someone upstairs hated me, but I felt a lot calmer discussing it with the dentist and made a plan for future appointments. I couldn't sit in the chair with the dentist leaning over me for longer than thirty minutes at a time, but if I raised my hand, he would stop working and let me get up for a minute. The dentist didn't display any surprise at my request, and I wondered if my mother had phoned ahead and warned him about my possible meltdown in the chair.

It was a painful and expensive experience but suddenly it's over and I'm good to go for another year. Something which gave me great relief and another reminder of what you can do when you put your mind to it.

Patrick must have felt dreadfully sorry for me in the middle of it all. I was exhausted with juggling everything and the pressures at work and home left me looking and feeling like a bit of a train wreck. I wasn't much joy to be around. One Friday evening he told me he had a surprise out the back for me: a nine-month-old-ish golden Labrador retriever called Buddy who needed a new home.

Chapter Thirty-Two

I was so happy I could have cried. I was speechless and delighted with him. We woke our son to come downstairs and he was super excited, but we left our daughter, who doesn't take too kindly to being woken. Buddy is a beautiful dog. Wonderfully big and gentle and looking nothing like Charlie Brown. He was full of excitement at his new surroundings and I knew instantly he would be very happy with us and we would be very happy with him. Our other dog was a bit put out but it was only for show – she had been dying with loneliness since Charlie Brown had gone and it only took a couple of days for them to become firm friends and for her to have a bit of life about her again.

I absolutely loved going out walking with Buddy and delighted in all the grooming and training that came with a new animal, and although I had yet to hear him bark I slept soundly for six wonderfully undisturbed hours safe in the knowledge that he was downstairs and hoping that should anyone try and enter our house, he would tell us so we weren't caught unawares. The children were madly in love with him, most especially our daughter, whose behaviour improved almost overnight as she had something new to focus her attention on, and Patrick had earned a massive amount of brownie points with his latest act of kindness.

Buddy went a long way to restoring the balance on my insides and I evened out a bit just in the nick of time for my trip to the big smoke which was causing me great anxiety. I got in touch with Julie to ask about meeting up and that opened a can of worms about my future involvement in the case. Apparently there was a scheme available to all victims, which wasn't up and running in my day, where you could register your details to be informed of any upcoming parole board hearings. You would then have the option of attending the hearing or giving a statement.

He was still in prison, having served almost ten years of His sentence, but was eligible to apply for parole under licence soon, and Julie asked me if I wanted to be part of the hearings or the procedure. I would be informed of the date of the hearings, the outcomes and should He have to apply more than once. I was instantly disturbed by the whole process. I wished I could give Judy a buzz to discuss it but I took my time and thought it over as to whether it would benefit me in the long run.

I had worked hard at severing any connection to Him that I might have in the future or had in the past, and I didn't wish to be involved with Him in the future. I felt I'd done more than enough to keep Him from harming anyone else, and I really didn't know how I would cope with the knowledge He was free to reoffend. I had changed so much over the last ten years that I was unrecognisable as the person I was back then. Maybe He had changed a lot too, hopefully for the better. I wouldn't feel comfortable making a suggestion as to whether He should stay in prison or not, and the advance knowledge of planned hearings would only add to my anxiety.

After much deliberation I decided, no, I didn't want to be involved and I didn't want to be part of any future decisions regarding His fate. I had let Him go in as many ways as it was possible and I decided to just leave it at that. Julie also asked me if I would be willing to share my story with other professionals at a training course they run for people working with victims of sex crimes. That was something I could be interested in if there were more hours in the day or a few extra days in the week, but I told her I would think about it and get back to her.

Phil said yes to coffee. It would be good to see each other. I finalised the plans for my trip: arriving at Stanstead on the Friday night, Rachel would pick me up at the airport. I would stay with her in my old room on Friday night before Anne arrived in London on Saturday. I'd go for a little trip down memory lane on Saturday, back to the flat and then head to the party on Saturday night. Anne and I would stay in a hotel that night and meet Phil on Sunday before arriving home on the Monday with it all behind me and me in one piece – I sincerely hoped.

I would be back to spend the Tuesday with the P man and our children who would surround me and share the love and light I needed to get through the anniversary unscathed once again. What a difference a decade made and how things had changed for me over the years. I wondered how things had changed in London too. I drove myself to the airport, heading up the motorway by myself for the first time in years. There was such heavy rain it was difficult to drive and I was tempted to turn the car around and go home again, but I pushed on through it and before I knew it I was in the air and saying goodbye to Belfast.

Rachel was waiting at the other end, and it was with such joy that we embraced. It had been almost three years, and many changes, since we had seen each other last. We caught up on the car journey, and it was surreal to be back in her home but it held nothing but pleasant memories for me and reminded me how safe and secure I felt there on the first few days after The Terrible Tuesday. Rachel and David had long since divorced and she was happy again with a new partner. I felt so welcome and slept soundly after a couple of glasses of vino and a lot of giggles reminiscing over old times. Saturday brought lots of rain but we went for a nice walk and I was overwhelmed by the hustle and bustle of Harringay with it being so long since I had been in a city. I found it noisy and it gave me a headache. I struggled to remember what I enjoyed about inner-city living. I had turned into a country bumpkin and missed the peace and quiet of home and the space inside my house and in the garden. Rachel's partner kindly drove me across to the hotel via the flat but it took so long to get from A to B with the traffic that I ran out of time to revisit the place properly.

We pulled up on the high street and I was instantly struck by how much it had changed. It was a lot cleaner looking with nice shops and a new tube station that made it a bit cooler and had put it on the map, but my heart felt like it had jumped out of my body so loud was my heartbeat when we turned down my old lane. We passed the ATM where he withdrew money with my bank card and pin number, drove down past the Chinese nail bar I used to go to and where the Chinese lady told me I had got very fat when I'd given up smoking, a statement that had me popping into the shop on my way home for a pack of twenty. Suddenly we were on my street. Rachel's partner pulled the car in and I got out for a look around.

I took a couple of deep breaths and walked towards the flat, struck by how little it had changed. The building looked exactly as it had done and I went in through the gate to find the front garden the same too. The pond was still there and the flowers were in bloom just as I remembered – it being the same time of year I legged it across the road to the nuns' house. I looked down the steps to the flat and see bars at the window and the front door. Apart from that it looked like I had stepped back in time. My heartbeat settled back down and I just felt an overwhelming sadness standing there thinking about my worst day and, more importantly, my escape from the darkness that seeped into my bones in the bedroom.

As I stood there getting soaked to the skin, the one thing I didn't feel was fear. It was strangely absent from my belly and chest and I felt a bit like Dorothy from *The Wizard of Oz* when she finally realised the witch had no power over her any more. All it was was a sad space in time. A terribly sad space in time which held no fear over me and it was with relief I realised I was finally free. I felt like crying but I didn't give in to it. I looked over at the nuns' house and realised I didn't have time to visit. Anne would be coming into Old Street soon but, honestly, I wasn't sure I had it in me to just knock the door and say, 'Hi, it's Alana. Do you remember me?' to whoever answered, and I'd faced enough demons for one day.

I got back into the car and Rachel's partner asked if I was all right. I said, yes, I was fine and I mostly was. A bit star-struck by it all but not shitting myself or anything remotely like it, which was only a good thing. We drove past what used to be our local watering hole, and, again, I couldn't believe it too looked the same. I was reminded of the many nights we spent there, drinking and having a laugh with friends. That was a good thought to be leaving the area with, and I made an effort to remind myself of all the things I loved about living there and how much fun Phil and I had together. I thought about how much I loved my work too, and what a shame my time there ended so badly and so abruptly.

I checked into our hotel and walked down to the station to meet Anne, deciding to pop into a nearby pub with a dodgy name but a nice vibe. I got a beer and sat by the window so I would see her arrive. I was lost in my thoughts when a youngish looking guy asked if he could join me. I was so taken back I said, no, I was waiting on someone. He said we could wait together and again I said no. He laughed at me and told me to stop being so rude, that he was only trying to make conversation. I apologised for forgetting my manners and he joined me, dragging my thoughts into the present. We were soon joined by another couple of fellas from Germany.

I was so uncomfortable and wondered what my children were doing at home while I was sitting in a bar in London talking to random strangers. I hoped they weren't serial killers planning to kidnap me, and it took all my reserves of strength to sit there and not panic at the prospect of something going seriously wrong.

Anne's flight had a lengthy delay, so I had no choice but to wait it out. When she finally arrived I breathed a huge sigh of relief that I would have her with me for the remainder of my trip. We were seriously late for the party but better late than never. I was so emotional to see Rachel's daddy and so glad I made it to the party. It was lovely to see Rachel's family and friends again and we had a lovely wee night catching up and doing a bit of dodgy dancing. I will forever remember Rachel's dad's surprise and delight at seeing us and will hold the memory of it in my head as another magical night.

I was more nervous than I cared to admit on Sunday morning as we headed to Islington to meet Phil. I wondered how it would all go. We spent a lot of lazy Sundays in Islington when we lived in London: walking, drinking coffee and reading the papers before heading for lunch, a couple of beers and a nice walk along the canal back in the days when we didn't even appreciate our child-free, stress-free existence, and I thought it would be a nice place to meet up. Anne headed for coffee and I went to the station to meet him.

I saw him walking towards me and suddenly I started to cry, properly cry, and I wasn't sure why or if I could stop but it made no difference anyway. He was very emotional too and we hugged each other for a long time. Again, I was overwhelmed by sadness. He looked the same as he did ten years ago and was as funny as I remembered him. We met with Anne and went for lunch, catching up with everyone's news, before heading to meet Rachel's family for the Ireland—France game in Shoreditch. I'd forgotten how annoying he was about any sort of sport that involved England or Ireland – him being an avid England fan and me an avid Ireland one, and it made for good craic throughout the day despite Ireland getting beat.

We headed over to Rachel's dad's to spend a bit more time with him and then go back to Islington, deciding to go for dinner before he caught the train back to Essex. We had a chance to talk about the end of our relationship, and he shared some of his own aftermath from The Terrible Tuesday. We both had regrets about how things ended between us and were both sorry we couldn't find a way to support each other through the dark days. I told him it was difficult to wish that day away now because I was so happy with Patrick and the children, and whatever I thought about it all and however challenging it had been, it was the path that led me to the deepest love I'd ever experienced and that becoming a mother was the best thing that had ever happened to me. Phil was as equally happy in his own life with his partner and their children, but we acknowledged it was the most difficult of journeys for each of us that ultimately led to our happiness.

We were both so upset and it was hard to say goodbye properly so choked was I with tears. We resolved to keep in touch this time and maybe meet up again soon with our partners and children. I walked back towards the hotel and phoned Patrick on my way. I just needed to hear his voice and I cried down the phone, although it was difficult to explain why I was so upset. I knew a proper conversation would have to wait until I got home, but he told me all about the kids and what they had been up to in my absence. I missed them all so much it was an ache in my chest.

I was emotionally exhausted but also felt a weight had been lifted from my shoulders having achieved everything I set out to over the weekend and having cleared the air with Phil. It was so good to see him, sad but also good, and I felt better about our parting than I had done for a long time. Anne was asleep as soon as her head hit the pillow but I lay there thinking over the events of the weekend. Her gentle snoring reminded me of sharing a room with her at the trial and as I lay there listening I realised it was almost time for home, and I was looking forward to the 'Welcome To Belfast' sign.

Chapter Thirty-Three

Monday seemed never-ending between the tube, the train, the plane and then the car, and it was with relief in my stomach that I finally pulled into the driveway to be greeted by two very excited children, two very excited dogs and one very relieved looking Patrick. I was truly blessed to have such a wonderful little family. I had missed them and I had missed home so much, it cemented my feelings that I could never live anywhere else again – green fields, mature trees and nice clean air were a must-have for me. The children had so much to tell me that it was non-stop chatter until bedtime. I had never been away from them for so long and it was vital that I heard every single thing they had done in my absence. Patrick was relieved I was back and had it all behind me. He regretted not coming with me, but I told him that wasn't the right time for him to be there, and the next time we will go together and visit London and see the city's sights like proper tourists and catch up with old friends. I could do that now I had my first return trip behind me – and I think I could have a good time.

Tuesday morning rolled around bright and early and I was immediately grateful for my own bed and the man beside me. The children clambered in with storybooks and we had some time to ourselves to read and just be comfortable with each other before heading downstairs for breakfast. I always make sure I'm up and about before nine in the morning – I'm never comfortable being in bed between the nightmare hour of nine and ten. That morning I was in a good mood with no anxiety in my belly. All I felt was sadness, and I was unsure if it would ever leave me. Sadness I can cope with though – it's almost a pleasure over every other emotion I'd experienced in the past.

We had a lovely morning: Patrick went to the bakery for fresh bread and the children had a bun after breakfast, unheard of in our house to have sugar so early in the day, but afterwards we headed to the lakes for a walk with the dogs and to see Charlie Brown's tree and I knew they'd burn it off in the fresh air. Charlie Brown's tree was getting bigger and had flowers on it which warmed my heart, and I was so touched when my son picked lots of flowers and arranged them in a circle around the tree asking if Charlie Brown would see them from heaven. I assured him Charlie Brown certainly would before we headed for a nice walk and Buddy a swim.

Patrick had some work to do, so I took the kids to my parents' house for it felt like an age since I'd last seen my mother even though it was only a couple of days. We passed an hour drinking tea and catching up on the weekend's events. Afterwards I sent a message to the girls – I'd been thinking of them and regretted that we no longer spent much time together. I remembered how I'd thought about them all in what I thought were my last moments all those years ago and I wanted to spend more time with them. It felt good to touch base and I resolved to make time to be more sociable.

We headed to the florists in the afternoon and picked up a nice bunch of flowers for Judy with the thought of popping into the centre to say hello. The calm atmosphere and familiar smell brought me right back to my first appointment – arriving with sunglasses on, stinking of smoke, so nervous I could hardly speak and so tired I could hardly stand up straight; so worried at finding myself at therapy and not knowing what would happen between us. I was struck, again, by how grateful I was to be ten years into my recovery.

I thought of all the wonderful people who had crossed my path and shared their light with me, for whatever length of time, and how it had given me the strength I needed to keep pushing on. I thought of the various dips in the roads, times when I had doubted my ability to make a full recovery, and of how I had been lifted, quite literally, through those times with an outpouring of love and light from my family, friends, Patrick and my children. I couldn't even begin to say how grateful I was for Judy, the centre and the part they played in my recovery. It was truly wonderful to see her again and to have the children with me, my most important little people. We hugged and she asked if I was okay. I told her I was, truly okay. That the road remained challenging at times but I was pushing on through. I had to, I had no choice, and my two little people were the main reason. I wanted them to know that nothing was impossible, that nothing life threw at you was impossible to overcome as long as you kept pushing through.

I told her I was still working on my manuscript, without her input this time, and that it was going okay. I was almost finished and determined to complete it as a project, mainly for my children. In the future I will be more than just 'Mummy'; in another ten years I hope we'll be friends as adults, and this manuscript will be my testament to a really difficult time I had before they were born, how I worked my way through the darkness and how they helped me. Judy couldn't get over how big the kids were and it was a reminder that time has a habit of moving on quickly when you want it to slow down. I thought back to watching the clock at the kitchen table, shaking and trying valiantly to hold myself together. Wondering how I would make it when time wouldn't move quickly enough for me, when one second dragged on into the next and I felt every painful tick as it moved. I couldn't wait for time to speed up through the most painful of minutes – which it just wouldn't do, but now I want it to slow down enough for me to enjoy my little people, enjoy my life and take a breath.

Time is man-made; it doesn't exist in spirit. It is people's measuring system, but when you break down into days and hours the cycle of the seasons and time passing, all that really matters is enjoying the love and light that comes your way and you keep pushing through the dark days. Whether your journey takes a year, ten years or twenty, the important thing is not to give up and not to give in. I believe that if I keep pushing I'll find a way through whatever challenges lie ahead of me just as I have done with those in my past. I'm overwhelmed with emotion to be sitting in the waiting area and grateful I'm not waiting on an appointment.

We said our goodbyes and I promised to pop in and see her when I'd completed my project. I can't wait to share it with her and think she'll laugh when she reads how close I'd been to picking up the phone and begging for an appointment. But she'll be proud of me for pushing on through and gathering myself again to move forward in my life. The kids and I met Patrick for dinner in a local restaurant and head home with the realisation that it had been a pleasant day for me. Phil and I had been in touch throughout the day and I felt a million times lighter now we had made our peace. I was decidedly grateful and also glad to see the back of the anniversary for another year.

Back at work there was a new post advertised within my team: a practice educator post. It was the same hours and money but with more of a focus on teaching and training and less on frontline nursing. I thought it was something I'd enjoy doing and would take me nicely in a new direction within nursing. I filled out the application form, without stressing too much at the thought of another job interview, and patiently awaited the interview date knowing I would be prepared, and if it was for me it wouldn't pass me, as my mother was so fond of saying.

I was prepared as I would ever be when the interview date came. I did a nice meditation about creating success with the success angel from a lovely angel therapist I found online before I left the house. I'd been listening to her meditations for a while and found them therapeutic and always felt clearer and lighter when I'd finished. I was nervous but not nausea nervous and the interview went well. I was delighted when they offered me the job later in the day, and I thanked the angels most sincerely for the new start that had appeared. I was relieved I'd be focusing more on teaching and training in my new role rather than the clinical aspect of nursing.

The house was progressing nicely and had been a learning curve for Patrick and me as we negotiated our way through fixtures and fittings and all the stress that came with building a forever home without killing each other. The project was a lot more stressful for Patrick than it was for me as he'd tried to do a lot of work himself to save us money and time on top of keeping his own business running. He had reached exhaustion and his heart was doing dodgy things again but we were almost at completion and he would have the winter months off to recover once we moved in and got settled. I was pleasantly surprised at how much I was looking forward to the move and took to the dreaded packing of boxes with an enthusiasm I didn't think was possible second time round, although I was safe in the knowledge this would be the last time I moved house for the foreseeable future.

I was especially excited about the space I'd allocated for my new den and was looking forward to unpacking my things and doing my first meditation. Initially it would just be for me to keep the balance on my insides, but I hoped to work with clients once we all got settled. I felt safe in the knowledge I would always have my own space to continue my shamanic and energy work with the angels and somewhere to just have a bit of space and time for myself.

Things had improved at home and our couples counselling had been helpful in realising we each brought different skills to the table and everything flowed better when we were on the same team instead of trying to manage on our own within the same household. Our approach to parenting was a lot more consistent and our children benefited from it. The meltdowns were getting less and less traumatic as time went on, and we found a wonderful woman for our daughter to work through her issues with. We watched her improving with such joy every day, and I was thankful she was a lot happier and seemed to be enjoying life more and more.

Life continued to improve and I got to spend a bit more time with the girls in the run-up to a wedding. I enjoyed the company of my friends immensely – a throwback to the child-free stress-free years when all I had to worry about was what I was going to wear and what to do with my hair before the big day. I realised there was such joy to be found in the little things in life – in spending time with people who make you laugh and warm your heart.

I had forgotten my promise to myself all those years ago when I said I would never again sweat the small stuff and would always remain grateful for my second chance at life. I guess it took working through another round with the darkness to remind me of it. I'll always hold tight to my mantra that if I never give up, I'll never be defeated, but on my journey through life, with all its ups and downs, the periods of darkness that came my way were always followed swiftly by periods of light and love, and I thought about what I would change about my life if I could.

There was nothing I would change, not one experience or one day, if I had the opportunity to do so for each one led me to experience something greater and something deeper and more meaningful than the one before. On a particularly challenging day I was in the middle of a tug of war and it was difficult to remain on the side of the light, but I told myself just to hold tight somewhere in the middle and not get pulled backwards into the sea of darkness. Some days it was easier than others but I wasn't afraid of asking for help when I needed it.

I thought right back to the beginning when I had no plan to get me through and it was impossible to decide which aspect of my recovery helped me most, which bit was the key to turning the corner, which bit I couldn't have done without. I actually couldn't single out one particular part. I thought it over for a while and then decided it was most definitely my mother. I couldn't have done it without my mother, but then it was also my father. God knows where I would be without my father. Then I thought it was also my brothers and sisters and my wonderful friends. It was also most definitely Judy. It was my shamanic work. It was giving evidence at the trial. It was Charlie Brown. It was my cottage. It was meditation. It was energy work. It was the angels. It was most definitely Patrick, most definitely my son and most definitely my daughter, and then it dawned on me: it was also me.

It was how I pushed myself through every challenge and every day and how I committed myself wholeheartedly to my recovery. It was never giving up, never giving in and being patient and taking my time to heal deeply and properly. It was recognising that I needed all the help I could get and gratefully accepting it along the way. It was being open to developing spiritually and not being afraid to face the demon. It was finally realising that everything I needed for my recovery was inside, and most importantly it was a combination of all the people and all my experiences that pushed me on through it. It was not the drama and chaos that seemed to surround me, or the challenges that came my way, that were important in my life. What was important was how I felt about them and how I reacted to them. I realised a long time ago that all I could do was change how I felt about my life, about The Terrible Tuesday, and the ups and downs the and highs and lows that happened since it and as a result of it, and this time, although I remained grateful, I chose joy.

I came across a picture in a quaint shop in Donegal town that said: *Your Journey is Exquisite: Choose Joy*. I bought it for a dear friend who I thought would appreciate the sentiment and it stuck with me. I thought, yes, my journey is exquisite. It was horrendous in some parts and magnificent in others. It had been filled with every emotion known to man as I travelled from extreme darkness back towards a life filled with light. It had been very difficult at times but I surprised myself with my determination and stamina to go the distance and stay on the right side of things.

When I thought back to the past, I thought of all the joyous experiences I had for they were the ones that outweighed the dark days and they were the ones that enriched my soul and gave me the strength to carry on and work through whatever experiences, challenges and blessings life had in store for me. For now, there is no anxiety in my belly and no fear in my body, and I find that a miracle in itself. For now, I am choosing to find joy in every experience that comes my way.

About the Author

Alana Corry is a Practice Educator in Community Children's Nursing.

When The Terrible Tuesday occurred in 2006, she was a Specialist Nurse in the Bone Marrow Transplant Unit at Great Ormond Street Hospital for Sick Children in London.

She has since been on a journey of discovery from a severe post traumatic stress disorder utilizing various tools to aid her recovery.

Ranging from psychotherapy to shammanic practice, from meditation to energy work and working with the angels, a combination of which, has allowed her to move forward with her life.

She now works in Northern Ireland in the community children's nursing team and as an integrated energy therapist having done various courses along the way in spiritual development, shamanic practice, meditation, reiki, integrated energy therapy and healing with the angels.

She lives with her partner, two children and two dogs.

Printed in Great Britain
by Amazon